Debt, Deficits, and the Demise of the American Economy

Debt, Deficits, and the Demise of the American Economy

Peter Tanous
Jeff Cox

John Wiley & Sons, Inc.

Published by John Wiley & Sons, Inc., Hoboken, New Jersey.

Published simultaneously in Canada.

For general information on our other products and services or for technical support, please contact our Customer Care Department within the United States at (800) 762-2974, outside the United States at (317) 572-3993 or fax (317) 572-4002.

Wiley also publishes its books in a variety of electronic formats. Some content that appears in print may not be available in electronic books. For more information about Wiley products, visit our web site at www.wiley.com.

Library of Congress Cataloging-in-Publication Data

Tanous, Peter J.

Debt, deficits, and the demise of the American economy / Peter J. Tanous and Jeff Cox.

p. cm.

Includes index.

ISBN 978-1-118-02151-4 (hardback); 978-1-118-07202-8 (ebk); 978-1-118-07203-5 (ebk); 978-1-118-07204-2 (ebk)

1. Investments–United States. 2. Stock price forecasting–United States. 3. Business forecasting–United States. 4. Financial crise–United States. 5. United States–Economic conditions–2009- I. Cox, Jeff, 1951- II. Title.

HG4521.T319 2011

330.973–dc22

2011007560

ISBN 978-1-118-02151-4 (cloth); 978-1-118-07202-8 (ebk); 978-1-118-07203-5 (ebk); 978-1-118-07204-2 (ebk)

Printed in the United States of America

10 9 8 7 6 5 4 3 2 1

To: Ann, Chris, Helene, Will, Paul, Julie,
Olivia, Isabella, Lilly, & Ringo

—Peter Tanous

To: MaryEllen, for always believing;
and Mom and Dad, for always being there

—Jeffrey Cox

Contents

Foreword

Americans historically have always risen to meet every challenge. The issues of debt and deficits necessitate substantial changes in how our economy is managed. Many of the changes that need to be made are known to our political class. Many politicians, past and present, have not exhibited the will to tackle our looming budget crisis. Political careers last longer when the truly difficult issues are kicked down the road to future leaders. But as evidenced by the huge fiscal conservative movement spreading across the country since February 2009, Americans have the will to make sacrifices to strengthen our country and thus guarantee a prosperous future for our children and grandchildren. *Debt, Deficits, and the Demise of the American Economy* will better arm the reader to understand the corrective measures we need to insist on by our political leaders to address the issues that challenge our legacy of exceptionalism.

Peter Tanous and Jeff Cox in *Debt, Deficits, and the Demise of the American Economy* afford the reader a concise, easy-to-read account of how the United States—and much of the globe—has arrived at a tenuous crossroads of debt and unsustainable spending. The reader takes a journey through the history of how years of misguided and underfunded policies, here and abroad, have caused an historic addiction of central banks to low interest rates and easy-money "cures" for bubbles caused by low rates and easy money.

What I enjoyed most about *Debt, Deficits, and the Demise of the American Economy* is the use of unvarnished facts to quantify how mountains of debt will be an insurmountable obstacle to Americans' most cherished dynamic, a higher standard of living for successive generations, if not addressed expeditiously. Messrs. Tanous and Cox illustrate how flawed policies in banking, housing, taxation, and regulation all contributed to the credit crisis of 2008. More importantly, how the growing gap between what government collects and what it spends has created a negative spiral of corrosiveness that threatens the financial solvency of global economies big and small.

The methodologies of the Office of Management and Budget, used by our leaders to handicap solutions to lowering long-term deficits, are broken down into easy-to-understand assumptions. The reader is given a simple view of how "guesses" of future inputs like growth, inflation, and interest rates may not reflect future realities. Even small miscalculations of such variables can lead to much larger deficits.

Simple questions like how an average American defines inflation versus a how a central banker does are broken down and addressed not only in terms of pricing realities but also in terms of investing realities. Is gold a good hedge against policies that weaken the purchasing power of our currency? How does the risk of a weaker dollar affect investment strategies? Can we invest during times of economic crisis profitably, effectively? All these questions are addressed in a fashion that strips away the nonessential economic jargon, leaving the readers better armed to protect their personal finances during these trying economic times.

—Rick Santelli
CNBC On-Air Editor and former member of the
Chicago Board of Trade and Chicago Mercantile Exchange

Introduction

The problem we now face is the most extraordinary financial crisis that I have ever seen or read about.

—Former Federal Reserve chairman Alan Greenspan (August 7, 2010, interview in the *New York Times*)

At age 84, Mr. Greenspan has been around the block a few times and is drawing on a lengthy history.

The United States is heading toward a financial catastrophe that will paralyze the country and lead to an extended period of economic mayhem and distress. The problems are not about politics anymore, not about Republicans and Democrats, not about the Fed or the Treasury or the shaky euro. It is too late for any practical initiative to stop it.

To reduce this to its simplest elements, the pending economic catastrophe is about debt, deficits, and inflation. We hope to demonstrate that the rising and unsustainable debt in Europe and the rising deficits in the United States will lead to potentially catastrophic consequences. At the top of the list is our contention that severe inflation lies ahead. We also intend to point the way to some investment strategies to help counter the negative effects of the financial crisis that is coming.

This book tells a story about what has happened to get us where we are, how the crisis is unfolding, and how it will likely end with a stock market crash. The timing is always difficult to predict, but the direction of the crisis is not. The trend is predictable because the crisis is proceeding along a linear path.

This is not the first book about predicting some event in the unknowable future. Indeed, most predictions are wrong simply because no one has come up with a good way to predict the future. That said, some events are more predictable than others.

Many of you have read the book *The Black Swan* by trader and philosopher Nassim Taleb, who one of us (Tanous) happens to know and respect enormously. At a gathering we both attended, Nassim made some brilliant comments about what is predictable and what isn't. Let's consider something that is predictable. Nassim pointed out that the maximum amount of calories most humans can consume in a single day is about 4,000. With that knowledge, he pointed out that we can safely predict how much that individual would weigh at the end of the day. At that same rate, a hungry person would eat about 28,000 calories a week. We might also predict just how much that person would weigh at the end of a week given his level of physical activity. There is little the individual could do on any given day that would make a difference in the weekly outcome. So we can predict events like how much a person will weigh in a day or a week given an intake of a known number of calories because the progression is knowable and linear.

Can we similarly predict with accuracy what the stock market will do tomorrow? No.

In the case of investments, there are no shortages of predictions of what the market will do tomorrow, next week, next month, and next year. But how accurate can they be? Not accurate at all. Taleb recounts the story of his early days as a trader when one of his colleagues pointed to another trader on the floor who had been very successful, accumulating a portfolio of $7 million over seven years. But in the crash of 1987, he lost it all in one day.

We can put a man on the moon; we cannot predict tomorrow's stock market.

In writing a book that involves predicting the future—and a stock market crash, no less—we are trying as best we can to adhere to what

Nassim Taleb refers to as *epistemic humility*. Most so-called stock market experts and economists engage in *epistemic arrogance,* which is the tendency to think you know more than you really do. By adhering to the principle of epistemic humility, we try to stick to predictions that are logical, visible, and linear so that the reader will readily sign on to where we are going and to the points we are making.

We have taken the liberty to write a book about the future because, as we will demonstrate, much of the information that leads to the future of the world's economies is indeed linear, and therefore predictable to some degree. For example, a nation that continues to accumulate debt will reach a level of total indebtedness where that nation's options become very limited, and also predictable. An analysis of the country's financial situation may well reveal that there is no reasonable prospect for repaying the debt. The available solutions are dire—devaluation, rescheduling, or some other form of default. And the financial mayhem that follows those events is also, sadly, predictable from history.

The crash will result from the piling on of events that will occur in the chronograph we will provide. The crash will occur as the world finally realizes that we have boxed ourselves into a financial corner with no way out.

What might happen? The stock market will decline by 2,000 to 3,000 points. A run on banks perceived to be weak will snowball into a banking crisis. Liquidity in the markets will come to a halt. Inflation will be rampant as the United States prints money to pay our debts and avoid a technical default.

In this work, the plan is to take you through the steps that got us here so you can judge the logic that leads to the conclusions we will reach. Please keep in mind that this book is not an economic treatise. The authors are versed in economics, finance, and the stock market, but neither of us is a professional economist. We will explain the crisis that is upon us in clear, understandable terms. You will not need to be an economist to follow the points and conclusions in this book.

Here's the payoff: If in the course of reading this book you are persuaded, as we are, that we are heading toward a financial calamity, you will want to prepare yourself financially to deal with the perils that lie ahead. We intend to point to specific investment strategies to counter the effects of higher inflation and the mounting fear that lurks in the not-too-distant future.

A final word about inflation (which will be covered in a separate chapter): Lest we think of inflation only in terms of our experience in the 1970s or, more drastically, in Germany's Weimar Republic, where wheelbarrows of cash were rolled down the sidewalk to buy a loaf of bread, look at this Zimbabwean banknote from 2008:

Yes, it is for 100 trillion dollars. Yes, it is real.
And it is worthless.

Chapter 1

It's the Deficit, Stupid

It is common knowledge that the United States owes a lot of money and that our debt is growing. No arguments about that. Where the debate starts and ends is how we are going to manage our debt. Will we be able to repay it? Will we choke on it? Or perhaps we will grow out of it and move into a surplus, much like we did during the Clinton administration.

First, the simple answer: The mounting U.S. deficit, i.e., the amount we spend over and above what we take in revenue and taxes, is a major problem that will result in a financial calamity soon. How soon? We don't know, but soon enough that we need to be prepared for it. Politicians often rail about the massive federal debt we are leaving to our children and our grandchildren. They are right about the debt and wrong about the timing. Our children and grandchildren will not have to deal with the problem; we will! The crisis is approaching at alarming speed, and that is what this book is about.

Let's back those statements up with some facts. Here again, we want to be conscious of the difference between epistemic humility and epistemic arrogance. Epistemology is a branch of philosophy that is about the study of knowledge. In our book, we try to distinguish between what is knowable and what isn't. The future by its nature is not knowable, but some things are easier to predict than others. Linear events are easier to predict than random events, which are unpredictable. For example, if you have a stack of books and you add a new book to the stack every day, it is fairly easy to predict how high your stack will be a month from now. As you read this book, we want to make the case that our predictions are solidly grounded. This will constitute epistemic humility. Epistemic arrogance, on the other hand, is to us the practice of predicting events that are not supported by existing facts or trends. That would indeed be epistemic arrogance.

It would be arrogant to proclaim exactly when our rising national debt will turn into a financial debacle and a stock market crash, but it will likely occur sooner than we think. The national debt consists of all of the securities, bonds, notes, and bills issued by the United States Treasury. As of December 31, 2010, the "total public debt outstanding" of $14.03 trillion was approximately 94 percent of annual gross domestic product (GDP) of $14.9 trillion.[1]

How High the Debt?

If today's national debt is at a scary high of nearly 100 percent of GDP, how does that compare to the levels of debt in our nation's history? As Figure 1.1 shows, we have come this close only once in the past. During World War II, the debt reached 120 percent of GDP. The debt was, of course, the result of the massive cost of World War II, and we spent quite a bit of time paying that down. After the war, expenses declined dramatically in the absence of the high cost of waging the war. As a result, the debt also came down. According to the president's budget for fiscal year 2010, the national debt will pass 100 percent of GDP in 2011, something that hasn't happened since the end of World War II.

Today, politicians and pundits rail about the massive deficits and the need to increase revenue and cut spending. Increasing revenue means raising taxes, something no politician wants to be accused of. Lowering expenses is an equally formidable challenge. Where do you cut?

Figure 1.2 shows where the money went in 2010. The shaded area to the right shows that over 50 percent of our budget expenditures are "mandatory" for things like Social Security, Medicare,

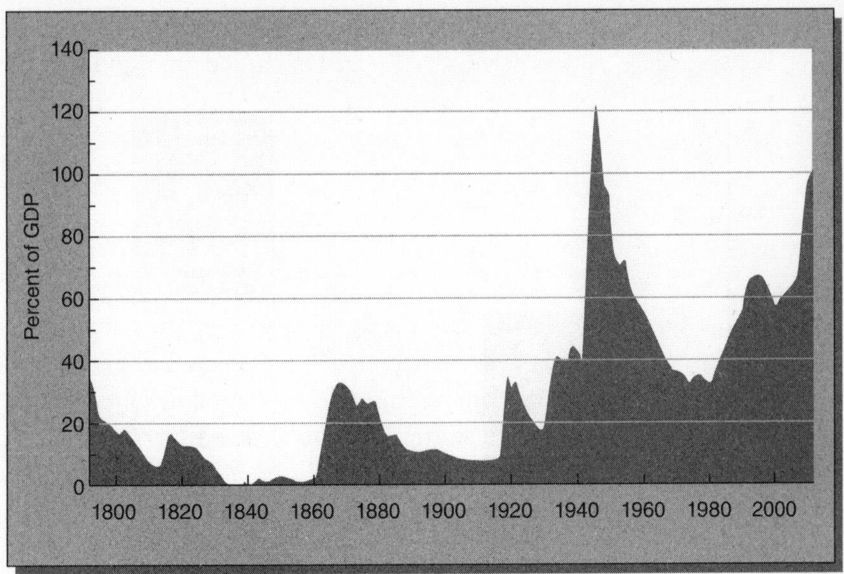

Figure 1.1 U.S. National Debt as Percent of GDP (Government Spending in the United States from 1792 to 2012)
SOURCE: usgovernmentspending.com.

Medicaid, and the interest on the national debt. These simply can't be cut. Of course, we can tinker with Social Security—by raising the age limit for retirees for example—but most politicians still treat Social Security as the third rail of politics: Touch it and you die.

The largest budget expenditure among the so-called discretionary spending categories is defense. Few politicians are eager to justify major cuts in defense spending, particularly in the aftermath of 9/11. That leaves very little room for making significant cuts.

So what about raising taxes? Here the debate gets heated. There is the constant reminder by Dr. Arthur Laffer (with whom one of us [Tanous] coauthored a book) that within certain limits raising taxes actually *decreases* tax revenue and lowering taxes *increases* tax revenue. The idea is that taxes are about incentives, so if you raise taxes, there is less incentive to take risk and if you lower taxes there is more incentive to work hard and take risk; hence more people working and building businesses results in higher tax receipts even if they are at a lower rate.[2] But no matter which side of that argument you take,

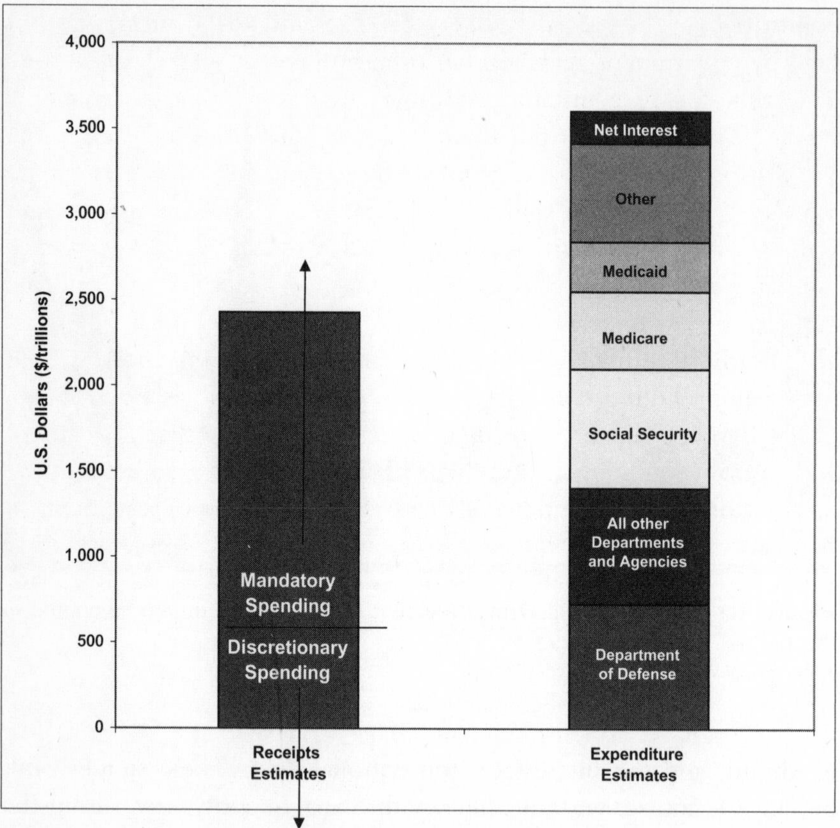

Figure 1.2 U.S. Receipt and Expenditure Estimates for Fiscal Year 2010

SOURCES: Congressional Budget Office and Lepercq Lynx Investment Advisory.

we all agree that raising taxes is hard to do, especially for politicians who have to agree to vote on it. If anything, this explains why it is so difficult to get out of the deficit morass. That is, until the deficit becomes a crisis and forces drastic action.

That is, of course, precisely what we see in our immediate future.

The Ticking Time Bomb

Sovereign debt issues in 2010 are estimated to total $4.5 trillion.[3] This sum is triple the amount of average debt issuance by developed countries over the preceding five years. U.S. total debt (including debt held by government agencies) has risen 50 percent since 2006 to over $14 trillion. These numbing numbers start to lose meaning after a while, at least until we put them in some other context.

To that end, let's have a look at the trend of U.S. debt in Figure 1.3. Keep in mind the source of this data, the Congressional Budget Office, which is nonpartisan. Although that doesn't guarantee that its estimates will be right, it does ensure that the projections will not be tainted by political bias.

Clearly, the trend is scary. According to these projections, which may well prove too conservative, U.S. debt (external) as a percentage of GDP will attain 90 percent in 2020. We believe that benchmark will come even sooner. And what happens when a country's debt reaches the level of 90 percent of GDP? (To avoid confusion, let us reiterate that there are *two* ways that federal debt is reported. One includes the internal debt such as borrowings by the government from the Social Security fund, which is essentially internal bookkeeping. The second method involves only the U.S. external debt held by the public and foreign governments.)

Economist Carmen Reinhart, who with Kenneth Rogoff co-authored the highly praised book *This Time It's Different: Eight Centuries of Financial Folly* (Princeton University Press, 2009), made the point of how heavily debt weighs on GDP. In an interview with *Forbes* magazine, Reinhart discussed her finding that a 90 percent ratio of government debt to GDP is a tipping point in economic growth. When government debt crosses that 90 percent line, the economy of the country in question has a growth rate that is 2 percent lower than an economy that has less debt.[4]

This is a significant point. As the United States approaches a debt level of 90 percent of GDP, if history holds and we subsequently have a 2 percent lower rate of growth, our growth *will not be strong enough* to sustain full employment and service our debt. This will further exacerbate and accelerate the debt crisis.

Table 1.1 shows the Congressional Budget Office (CBO) estimate of the projected total deficits through 2020. Its estimates are arguably optimistic. As bad as these estimates look, the reality is that they will

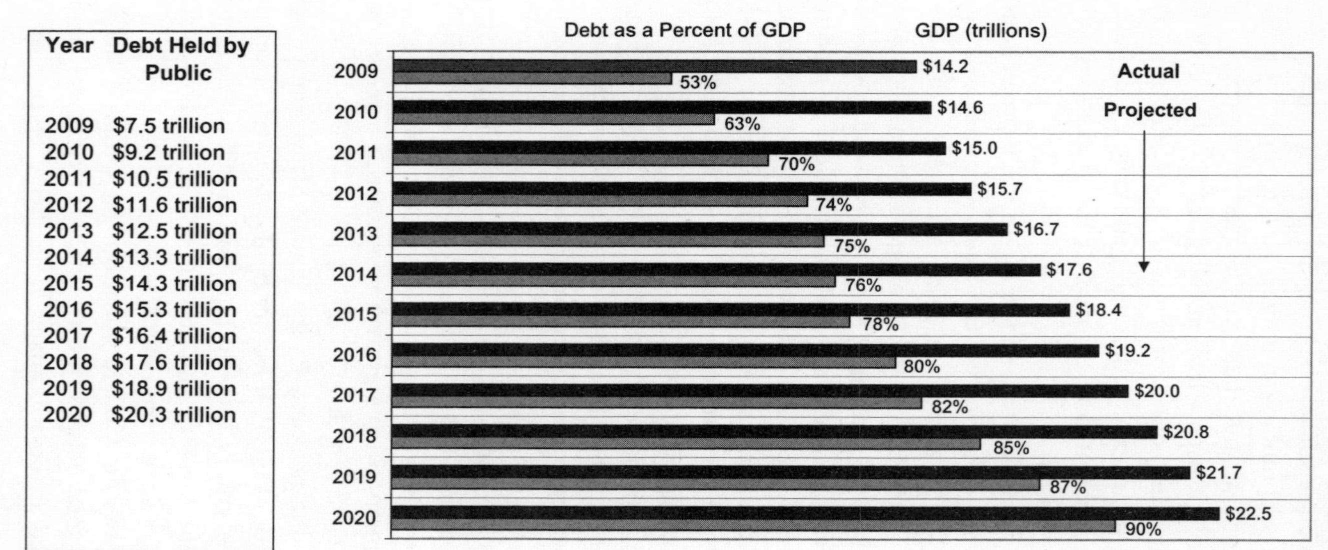

Year	Debt Held by Public
2009	$7.5 trillion
2010	$9.2 trillion
2011	$10.5 trillion
2012	$11.6 trillion
2013	$12.5 trillion
2014	$13.3 trillion
2015	$14.3 trillion
2016	$15.3 trillion
2017	$16.4 trillion
2018	$17.6 trillion
2019	$18.9 trillion
2020	$20.3 trillion

Figure 1.3 Debt Compared with the Gross Domestic Product
SOURCE: Congressional Budget Office.

Table 1.1 CBO's Estimate of the President's Budget (billions)

	Actual 2009	2010	2011	2012	2013	2014	2015	2016	2017	2018	2019	2020
Revenues	2,100	2,100	2,500	2,800	3,000	3,300	3,500	3,700	3,900	4,000	4,200	4,400
Expenses	3,500	3,600	3,800	3,700	3,800	4,000	4,300	4,600	4,800	5,000	5,400	5,700
Total Deficit	−1,400	−1,500	−1,300	−900	−800	−700	−800	−900	−900	−1,000	−1,200	−1,300

CBO's Year-by-Year Forecast and Projections

		Forecast		Projected								
	Est. 2009	2010	2011	2012	2013	2014	2015	2016	2017	2018	2019	2020
Nominal GDP (billions)	14,200	14,700	15,100	16,000	16,900	17,800	18,600	19,400	20,200	21,000	21,800	22,800
Nominal GDP (% change)	−1.3	3.2	2.8	5.6	5.9	5.3	4.5	4.3	4.1	4.0	4.0	4.1

Source: Congressional Budget Office.

prove overly optimistic. Here's why: According to the CBO, "federal debt held by the public will stand at 62 percent of GDP at the end of fiscal year 2010, having risen from 36 percent at the end of fiscal year 2007, just before the recession began. In only one other period in U.S. history—during and shortly after World War II—has that figure exceeded 50 percent."[5]

Looking at the bottom line of Table 1.1 (Nominal GDP, % change), the CBO rates of growth of GDP seem very optimistic to us and many others. The projected growth rates of GDP in 2012, 2013, and 2014 are all in excess of 5 percent, ranging from 5.3 percent to 5.9 percent. We don't think this is realistic. Most CBO original projections turn out to be wrong, but then again, almost all long-term economic predictions are wrong.

Remember that consumer spending accounts for nearly 70 percent of GDP. With unemployment stuck above 9 percent and consumer confidence relatively low, how likely is it that GDP is going to grow at very high rates? And if the growth isn't there, revenues will be lower than expected and the deficit will increase even faster. An aging population and much higher health care costs will push federal spending as a percentage of GDP *much higher*. What then?

The Rising Debt and the Rising Cost of Debt

In May 2010, Moody's—one of the major credit rating agencies—estimated that the cost of servicing the U.S. national debt could rise to as much as 23 percent of federal revenues by 2013, assuming much less optimistic assumptions about economic recovery than those published by the CBO.[6] When the debt servicing costs for a nation reaches 18 percent or more, that country is on the equivalent of a "credit watch" by the rating agencies. Indeed, none of the major credit agencies wants to see sovereign debt service in excess of 20 percent. If that happens, the credit agencies will downgrade that country's debt.

Might the United States seriously be in danger of a credit downgrade? Well, yes. Interest rates today are at or near all-time lows, so the cost of servicing the debt is also low. And, of course, the debt is rising perilously and, as we have seen, we risk an explosion of new debt as a result of the growing deficits. If interest rates rise, which we believe is certain to happen and which will be discussed in a later chapter, then we have the double negative effect of higher interest costs and higher debt adding to our overall costs of servicing the debt.

A downgrade of U.S. debt has never happened, but if it does, there is no doubt that such an event would send shock waves through the world of finance. No one can reasonably predict the outcome if a downgrade occurs, but it is sure to be ugly. (Think of plummeting prices of U.S. Treasury bonds and notes!)

Will the United States Default on Its Debt?

In a word, no. The United States doesn't ever need to default so long as our currency remains desirable and relatively safe. We always have the option of the printing press to make more currency with which to pay back the debt. As inflation lurks, we will wind up paying back our old debt with cheapened dollars. This scenario is widely discussed as a possible solution to our towering debt.

But is it realistic?

Here's the problem. About 40 percent of our federal debt is scheduled to mature by midyear 2011. Seventy percent of the debt will mature within five years.[7] If investors smell even a whiff of inflation, they will demand higher interest rates when the government attempts to roll over (reissue) the debt as it matures. And since so much federal debt is maturing within the next few years, it is very important to keep interest rates low in the short term. For a strategy of "inflating our way out of debt" to work, we would need to have a much higher proportion of long-term debt to short-term debt. Indeed, we can't inflate our way home if inflation causes us to roll over existing debt at much higher interest rates. Doing that just makes a bad problem even worse. Moreover, we also have TIPS bonds, which are Treasury bonds that adjust for inflation. These would react swiftly to a rise in inflation since the principal amount on these bonds is adjusted for inflation every six months. At this point, however, inflation-adjusted bonds (TIPS) account for only 7 percent of the total.

The fact that 40 percent of outstanding Treasury securities will mature in 2011 sets the stage for the crisis. But in our view, the chain of events leading to a world stock market crash will start not in the United States, but rather in Europe.

Chapter 2

The Crisis Begins

Perhaps you have heard of the PIIGS, the rather inelegant term referring to a group of countries with fabled pasts, long histories, and some of the most coveted tourist destinations in the world. PIIGS stands for Portugal, Italy, Ireland, Greece, and Spain. Today, the PIIGS also share a major common problem: They have more debt than they can afford to pay.

One of the features the PIIGS have in common is that they are all part of the eurozone, an economic union that uses a common currency, the euro. The euro was incubated in 1992 when European leaders signed the Treaty of Maastricht, which set the stage for a union of major European countries that would adopt the euro as their common currency. The euro itself entered into use in early 2002.

In this chapter, we will take you through a brief history of the euro, then move on to the unraveling of the eurozone and the problems with some of the countries' sovereign debt issues that started in 2010.

The Rise and Fall of the European Currency

Right from the start there were clearly two tiers of eurozone countries. On the one hand were the developed economic nations of

Austria, Belgium, France, Germany and the Netherlands, which we refer to as EUN. These were the established, mature economies of northern Europe, countries with stable economies and long-established institutions. The PIIGS comprised mostly southern European economies, and while these nations had long world histories (think of Greece) their economies and more recent history were not as established or trusted as much as those of their northern brethren. So it was certainly fair to ask how these disparate nations with widely divergent wealth, economic policies, and institutions might live and thrive together under a single economic union and currency.

In the beginning of the union, things worked out pretty well. In the early 2000s, stock markets endured three years of declines in the aftermath of the Internet boom and bust. The U.S. stock market declined three years in a row, from 2000 to 2002, after the euphoric Internet bubble burst in early 2000. European markets also fared poorly, but a broad economic recovery had begun and interest rates were low. Widespread confidence fueled a surge in consumer buying throughout Europe. Then the combination of low interest rates and rising demand led to a large increase in private debt.

This period of prosperity spread from the eurozone countries to several other members of the European Union that, while not part of the euro currency group, simply pegged their exchange rates to the euro. Among those countries that did so were Estonia, Lithuania, and Latvia. (Estonia adopted the euro in mid-2010.)

With rising borrowing and spending came rising prices. Wages in the PIIGS rose almost 6 percent per annum from 1997 to 2007 while the comparable wage increase in the EUN countries averaged only 3.2 percent. Had productivity risen more rapidly in the PIIGS countries, that might have mitigated the increase in wages, but productivity gains in the PIIGS were essentially the same as the gains in the more developed European nations. The result was that unit labor costs in that period rose by an average of 26 percent in Greece, Portugal, and Italy and rose only 17 percent in the rest of the eurozone, except for Germany, where wages went up by only 3 percent.[1]

Now if labor costs are rising much faster in some eurozone countries than they are in others, you can see the trouble coming: the countries with the fast-rising wages will have higher costs and higher prices, and their products will be less competitive. In the United States, during the housing bubble that lead to the Great Recession in 2008–2009, housing prices rose 4.6 percent per annum. Compare that growth to the housing price increases from 1997 to 2007 of 8 percent per annum in Spain and 12.5 percent in Ireland!

As prosperity thrived on the combination of consumer spending and low interest rates, tax revenues for the European governments also rose. Predictably (alas, it is true all over the world), when government revenues increase, so does government spending. In retrospect, what the European governments should have done was realize that these higher tax revenues were the result of a cyclical boom. With that understanding, they should have put some money away for a rainy day. But, of course, they didn't do that.

Figure 2.1 shows the annual growth of government expenditures in the eurozone countries from 1997 to 2007. Ireland leads the list with an astounding 10 percent annual growth in government

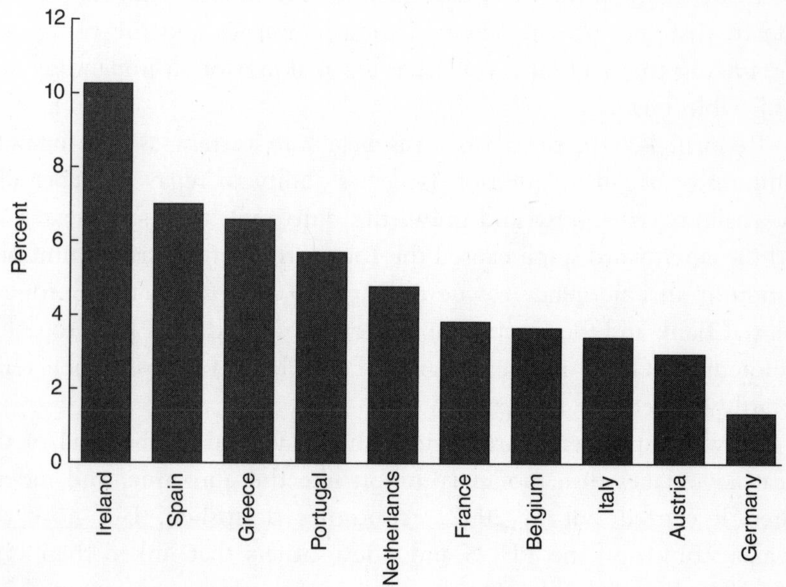

Figure 2.1 Annual Growth of Government Expenditure (percent average, 1997–2007)

SOURCE: Eurostat, "Paradigm Lost: The Euro in Crisis," paper by Uri Dadush/Carnegie Endowment for International Peace, 2010.

expenditures, and four of the PIIGS occupy the four top spots. The country with the least rise in government expenditures over that period was, not surprisingly, Germany, the most economically powerful country in the union.

Following this period of prosperity beginning in the late 1990s, a period of slower growth ensued. At many of the PIIGS, where spending by both government and the private sector was lavish and prices rose on the heels of high demand, the slowdown began. Portugal and Italy were first to feel the slowdown, and their deficits increased. Greece's fiscal mismanagement contributed to annual deficits of 5 percent of gross domestic product (GDP) starting in 2000. Under European Union rules, budget deficits may not exceed 3 percent of GDP.[2]

As the housing crisis, which hit the United States hard, spread to Europe, housing bubbles in Spain and Ireland became particularly severe and required large government interventions, exacerbating the deficits in these countries. The economic slowdown and rising costs also made many of the PIIGS less competitive in international markets. Add to that the growing debt in these countries and the rising cost of servicing the debt, and you have the makings of an impending and predictable crisis.

In spring 2010, the euro crisis began in earnest as the financial community began to question Greece's ability to repay its debt. The snowballing crisis grew and grew, the euro sank to a four-year low, and the downward spiral caused the International financial community to mount an emergency rescue package. In May 2010, the European Central Bank and the International Monetary Fund (IMF) put together a Herculean Greek rescue package of 750 billion euros, which temporarily calmed the markets.

Now the problem starts to take shape. We heard about all of the great advantages of a monetary union like the eurozone, and indeed when it started out in 2002, economies flourished. But now the weaker countries, the PIIGS and a few others that linked their currency to the euro, like Estonia, Lithuania, and Latvia, faced a big problem. In most countries that have their own currency, when an economic slowdown occurs, the central bank can adopt a number of measures to alleviate the crisis. The most common measure is to lower interest rates and make credit available to stimulate economic activity. *But the three little PIIGS, Greece, Spain and Ireland, which desperately needed to stimulate their economies, were unable to do so because they were part of the eurozone and had no control over interest rates!*

The Strong versus the Weak

By contrast, consider Germany's development since it joined the eurozone. Germany's exports have risen more than those of any other country in the European Union. In the process, Germany became the world's largest exporter. Since other regions of the world have grown faster than the eurozone in recent years, Germany's exports to the euro area have declined while increasing to other parts of the world.

A number of other characteristics have strengthened Germany's economy while many others in the eurozone have declined. Germany is the fifth largest economy in the world in purchasing power, according to the *CIA World Factbook* (2010). The country recovered smartly from the 2008 recession and expected GDP growth of 3.5 percent in 2010. However, not all of its neighbors are pleased with Germany's economic path. Germany is one of the most productive exporters in the world, which is, of course, good for German business. However, Germany's neighbors complain that Germany has not encouraged enough domestic consumption, which would benefit neighboring countries, which are net exporters.

The point we want to make is this: As some of the countries in the eurozone ran into serious economic problems, other stronger countries were experiencing growth and prosperity. Since they all shared a currency, though, the countries that needed economic solutions involving lower interest rates and looser monetary policy were unable to use these tools because they were a part of an economic and currency union whose member countries had widely disparate economic circumstances. Think of children who grow up in the same household. Years later, one of the kids is rich and famous, and the others are struggling. They may all want to fly to Tahiti for a family vacation, but only one of the siblings can afford to do so. Tension ensues.

In the past, when a country's economic situation got out of line through mismanagement, a spending binge, or other mistakes, the country had as a last resort the option to devalue its currency or worse, default on its debt. In recent times, we recall the case of Argentina, which adopted both of those drastic measures. Indeed, Argentina devalued the peso in 2002 and saw it decline by 70 percent against the U.S. dollar. The devaluation resulted in a default on 75 percent of Argentinean foreign debt. Argentineans suffered huge inflation, and many tried to change their currency into dollars. Unemployment rose. Mobs set fires and attacked businesses, especially American businesses like Coca-Cola. Drastic measures like that are not soon forgotten by the international financial community. Today, Argentina still has little or no access to the financial markets, and its Standard & Poor's rating is among the worst in the world.

Now the euro nations do not have the ability to devalue their currency since their currency is not their own, but one shared by 16 nations. (Unfazed by the crisis, Estonia adopted the euro currency in mid-2010.) Default, however, is still an option, but it brings terrible consequences for the other nations that share the currency. If one eurozone nation defaults, the financial community immediately turns its attention to the next weakest country. This is how the PIIGS got lumped together as a group of potentially worrisome debtors.

Preventing the Fire from Spreading

We tend to toss around words like "default" without digging deeper into what it might mean in particular circumstances. In the world of debt, a default simply means that a debtor does not meet its obligations, which include paying interest on time and paying the debt back at the maturity of the loan. But when nations talk about default, they tend to use less dramatic worlds like "restructuring" and "rescheduling," which sound more like changing a scheduled appointment than defaulting on your obligations.

Restructuring and rescheduling mean mostly the same thing. A debtor will announce that it is not going to pay back the loan under the original terms agreed upon. (That is, in fact, a default.) In a pure default, it will simply announce that it is not paying back the loan. Period. The more likely event is that a country will announce that it can no longer afford to pay the debt and is reducing the principal amount owed by, say, 50 percent. So if you lent this unfortunate country $1000, your debt is now worth $500, which is the new amount the country will repay you. Oh, and it may also decide to extend the maturity. You lent them the money for 5 years? Well, now you'll get repaid in 10 years. Finally, that interest rate they promised you was awfully high, wasn't it? So the promised interest rate of 8 percent is now reduced to 4 percent. Sorry.

And what can you do about it? Well, if you borrowed from a corporation, you and the other creditors would be entitled to put the corporation into bankruptcy and liquidate the assets to try to get your money back. Sell the factory, sell the land, auction off the other assets, and hope the proceeds will cover what you are owed. But in the case of sovereign debt, what do you do? Repossess the Parthenon? Not likely.

So investing in the debt of sovereign nations involves a range of risks and advantages. The advantage is that sovereign nations rarely default. The disadvantage is that when they do, there is not a lot you can do to get your money back. This is the beginning of the crisis. When investors become concerned about one or more countries' sovereign debt, you have the potential for a monumental crisis that could spread like a forest fire.

This process began with the Greek Crisis in mid-2010. In order to protect our assets and intelligently prepare for what is coming, we need to carefully analyze what is likely to happen next.

The Greeks Have a Word for It: Default

In December 2010, an IMF report on Greece estimated that Greek debt would reach € 347.2 billion in 2011, and that gross debt as a percentage of GDP would soar to 152 percent in 2011 from 141 percent in 2010 and 127 percent in 2009.[3] The country's interest payments are rising rapidly as a result of the mounting debt burden, and the higher interest rate investors are demanding to hold Greek debt. In 2012, by some estimates, Greece will be paying €17 billion in interest alone, up from € 12 billion in 2009.[4] Based on projections that may well prove optimistic, Greek debt will peak at about €350 billion in 2014, at which time the interest payments will be at least € 20 billion and probably much more due to the likelihood that interest rates will rise. The IMF projects that Greece will have to borrow €70 billion in 2014, if everything goes according to plan.[5]

The problem is both stark and simple: Greece's dire financial condition resulted in the imposition of harsh austerity measures as a condition of the massive loans by the IMF and the European Union that bailed the country out in May 2010 through the establishment of the European Financial Stability Facility (EFSF), which, along with the IMF, provided a € 750 billion safety net for member states. But those austerity measures virtually ensure that Greece will not be able to grow fast enough to earn the funds it needs to pay back the old debt and get the country back on a solid footing.

In late January 2011, a creative idea was floated in European financial circles to allow Greece to buy back its bonds at a discount. Given the flow of bad economic news emanating from Athens, Greek sovereign debt traded at a significant discount to their original issue prices. Indeed, in January 2011, Greek 10-year bonds traded at about 70 percent of their original issue price. So the EFSF would be wise to consider lending Greece the money to buy back its own bonds at a significant discount. Buying back Greek debt at a 30 percent discount from the issue price would reduce the country's debt burden by the same amount. However, there was some debate as to how much such a measure would help Greece. For one, this scheme requires sellers willing to take a big loss on their holdings of Greek debt. How many of those are there? One analyst, quoted in the *Financial Times* on January 20, 2011, stated that Greece would be able to save only € 12.5 billion on its debt through the buybacks, which would bring its estimated debt-to-GDP ratio in 2013 down from 158 percent to 153 percent, a barely noticeable improvement.[6]

So Greece is barreling down the track, headed straight to a train wreck.

Greece Will Default, but When? We Think We Know the Answer

Now let's consider when and how the next crisis will occur. There are some interesting clues and facts we can use to speculate on both the timing and the events that will inevitably unfold as Greece heads toward default.

First, we look at the nature of Greece's deficit. In 2009, for example, Greece had a primary deficit of € 20 billion. That means that before paying a single euro in interest payments, Greece was €20 billion short in covering its internal obligations, like pension payments, public services, and other necessary expenditures. Now it makes sense that Greece does not under any circumstances want to default if its budget is so bad that it can't pay the daily bills and keep the lights on and the buses and trains moving. It must get to the point where it can survive as a nation based on its internal budget, since after a default it will be highly unlikely that Greece will be able to borrow any money, including the funds to fulfill its internal obligations.

Based on the austerity measures imposed on Greece by the European Union and the IMF as conditions of the May 2010 rescue package (which was part of the € 750 billion IMF/EFSF package), Greece should be on a path to reduce its deficit so that by 2012 or a bit later the primary deficit of € 20 billion will have turned into a small surplus. Remember, the primary deficit *excludes* interest and principal payment on the country's debt. So if all goes according to plan, sometime in 2012, Greece will be able to meet all of its internal obligations. The trains will run on time, the lights will stay on, salaries will be paid, and all the other financial obligations of government will be met. But the remaining financial obligation is a very big one: servicing the external debt. By 2012, Greece will likely be spending €17 billion just to service the debt, and that sum will rise to an annual expenditure of over € 20 billion. To put that sum into context, € 20 billion is very close to the amount Greece will spend annually on government salaries.

Now, let's jump ahead to 2012 or 2013. You are the prime minister of Greece. You have to explain to your constituents, the Greek people, that while you recognize that they have suffered tremendously from the austerity imposed on Greece over the past three years, you must now spend an enormous amount of Greece's wealth to repay the debts owed to foreigners. Indeed, a series of Greek sovereign bond debt is maturing next week requiring the payment of principal of €1.5 billion. What might you do?

You confer with your cabinet and determine that the needs of the country are great. Schools are overcrowded, public servants have endured salary decreases and no subsequent wage increases in several years, roads and bridges are in such disrepair that they have become a safety hazard, and pension demands are rising and cannot be met under the austerity plan. And, oh yes, in addition to the € 1.5 billion payment now due, the country owes this year € 17 billion in debt service to the bankers of Europe.

The likely course of action seems painful, but obvious. Greece can meet its basic needs, but not for long. A restructuring of Greek debt will save the country at least € 10 billion a year and allow the country to recover. Restructuring is painful but, like growing old, the alternative is worse. A decision is made. The prime minister makes plans to phone the president of the European Central Bank to inform him of the decision while the minister of finance prepares the plan for the mandatory restructuring of the debt.

The initial thinking at the Finance Ministry is that a "haircut" of 35 percent of principal will be imposed, meaning that for every 1000 euros invested in Greek debt, the new face amount will be reduced to 650 euros. Debt maturities will be extended to 10 years, doubling the average maturity of the existing debt. Interest payments will be brought down from an average of 7.5 percent to 3 percent.

And so the crisis begins.

Erin Go Broke

Ireland was one of the pioneers of the euro, joining the currency union in 1999 and along with the 11 other nations who initially formed the eurozone, began employing it as currency when the euro started trading in 2002. The economic growth of Ireland in the 1990s is a legendary tale. The country had been one of the poorest in Europe when it transformed itself into one of the fastest growing in the world. A major contributor to Ireland's meteoric growth was a decision to lower the corporate income tax rate. At 12.5 percent, Ireland undercut the tax rate in the rest of the EU and attracted considerable new business. Other countries were furious, notably the French, who continually push the Irish to increase their corporate tax rate as part of their economic recovery. Ireland's growth was also fueled by Ireland's emergence as a financial center along with the growth of its banks and a corresponding real estate boom. The EU contributed to the economic miracle through huge transfers from the EU Structural and Cohesion Funds, which are the EU's policy instrument to even out the living standards among EU countries. Ireland soon became known as the Celtic Tiger. Between 1997 and 2007, home prices in Ireland rose by 400 percent.

In 2008 in the United States, the real estate bubble was in full burst mode. A major American investment bank, Lehman Brothers, was allowed to fail and a severe sense of panic prevailed throughout the financial community and beyond, right down to Main Street. About the same time, Ireland's real estate bubble also burst with dire consequences. The Celtic Tiger was whimpering.

Ireland's six largest banks soon faced the precipice. As the crisis unfolded, bad loans, mostly in real estate, devastated the portfolios of the largest Irish banks.

In late 2008, the Irish government was faced with an urgent decision: It appeared that several Irish banks were on the brink of failing. What to do? If one bank failed, there would be a run on the other weak banks and the entire financial system of the country would collapse. So the Irish government made a difficult decision: It guaranteed all of the liabilities of the six largest banks in Ireland at a cost of €400 billion. The amount was later bumped up to € 480 billion to cover the liabilities of some foreign-owned banks with major operations in Ireland.[7] This measure gave some temporary relief. Soon a stream of bad news started to flow from the Irish banks raising a new set of fear and concerns. Irish bank stocks tumbled over the following weeks. The government responded to the steep declines in Ireland's bank stocks by announcing it would invest up to 10 billion euros to recapitalize them.

In January, 2009, the Irish government declared it would invest an additional € 7 billion to recapitalize the two largest banks.[8] Later that month, the government announced plans to nationalize Anglo Irish Bank, the largest bank in Ireland. And the problems were still just beginning.

Over the following months, Ireland's financial condition worsened and so did the balance sheets of the Irish banks. Two more banks were nationalized. In October 2010, Ireland's minister of finance effectively nationalized the country's second biggest bank, Allied Irish Banks. As a result of the huge amounts of money used to bail out virtually Ireland's entire banking system, the country's budget deficit rose to 32 percent of GDP, or *ten times* the amount allowable by the European Union for its members.[9] Comments in the press called for withdrawal from the eurozone. Indeed, if Ireland had its own currency, it could help solve its problems by devaluing the currency.

By 2010, Ireland's 300,000 public-sector employees had endured a 15 percent average pay cut over the previous three years while the government's budget, once in surplus, declined dramatically into deficit.

Figure 2.2 shows the budget deficit approaching 32 percent of GDP in 2010. Ireland's plan is to get back to an allowable deficit of 3 percent of GDP by 2014. Of course, almost no one believes this will happen. In 2010, Irish unemployment rose to 13 percent.[10] An

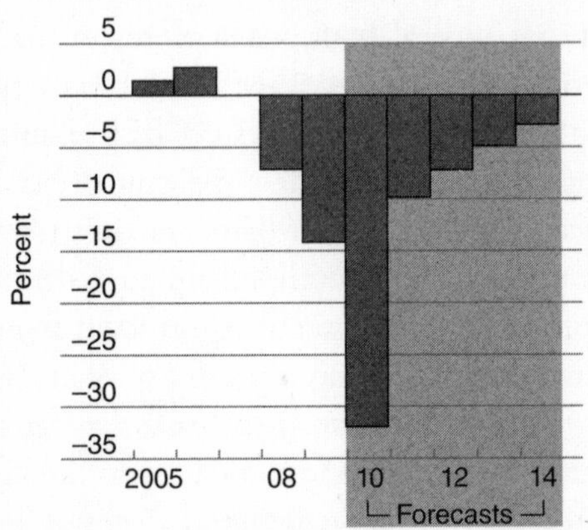

Figure 2.2 Ireland's Budget Balance (as Percent of GDP)
SOURCE: Irish government.

Irish think tank estimated that Ireland would need to save €15 billion to achieve the desired deficit of 3 percent of GDP by 2014.[11] No one could explain how a country with high unemployment and a contracting economy was going to save anywhere near that much. They won't.

In late 2010, Anglo Irish Bank, now effectively owned by the government, offered its junior debt holders an exchange of their €1.6 billion in bonds for new, government-guaranteed bonds. Not surprisingly, there was a catch. The new bonds would be worth about 20 percent of the value of the old bonds. Lower ranking holders of debt were offered 5 percent of the face value of their bonds. The bonds of one of the largest banks in Ireland were now worth pennies on the dollar, or to be more precise, the euro. How much worse could it get?

In Ireland, you had a government that during the good times relied heavily on consumption and real estate taxes. Anyone who believes that the Irish economy will recover swiftly must deal with the fact that in a land where unemployment (in late 2010) has reached 13 percent, consumption tax revenues are not likely to go up any time soon. And in a nation that had prospered from real estate taxes, it is not likely that a quick economic recovery and a resumption of real estate tax revenues will occur soon given that in this country of 4.5 million people over 150,000 homes stand empty.

Add to these depressing statistics the fact that, as we have seen, Ireland's financial system is in near ruins and the debt burden is mountainous. As 2010 drew to a close, a major rescue package for Ireland totaling € 85 billion was put together by the European Union. Irish bonds plunged while the interest rates on Irish debt soared to over 8 percent. Once again the precarious condition of the country's major banks was to blame. Is a recovery possible under these conditions? We don't think so. The solution is the same as it is for Greece. In order to begin a true economic recovery, Ireland must get its financial house in order and clear the way to a path for growth. To do that, the debt burden must be reduced to a manageable amount. And to do that, the country will have to restructure its debt. Remember that "restructure" is a polite term for default.

In late January 2011, the Irish government fell, adding more uncertainty to the country's precarious financial condition. At the risk of venturing into the unpredictable and at the risk of engaging in epistemic arrogance, let's take a guess as to when Ireland might default. So here it is:

Right after Greece!

The Pain in Spain

Writers often describe Spain with facile adjectives like "sleepy" and overuse words like "siesta" and "mañana." These outdated and insulting characterizations notwithstanding, nothing could be further from the truth. Spain, a nation of 46 million inhabitants, is a sophisticated, urbane, industrial nation right up there with the leading nations of Europe. But Spain's financial problems are of special concern because unlike Greece and Ireland, Spain is a large country. In terms of its economy and its GDP, Spain is the fourth largest nation in the eurozone and it is the 10th largest nation in the world. In short, Spain is simply too big to be bailed out. And sadly, Spain is teetering on the edge of bankruptcy.

As of the end of 2010, Spain was living through its worst recession in 60 years. Like Ireland and the United States, Spain suffered a massive housing meltdown, which led to a large drop in consumer spending, rising unemployment, and a steep decline in tax revenues. These conditions are not likely to be corrected quickly. Spain's debt-to-GDP ratio was about 65 percent in 2010 and expected to climb to 72 percent in 2011.[12] Its budget deficit, at 11 percent of GDP, is the third largest in the eurozone.[13] By now you will recall that under the rules and condition of the European Union, member states may not allow their budget deficits to exceed 3 percent. What can a country do in a perilous situation like this? In the old days before the euro, a country would simply devalue its currency and start over. But when your country is part of a 16-nation currency union, that choice is not available. All of the major credit rating agencies have downgraded Spain's debt.

The newest tool the EU possesses to help its member countries in trouble is the EFSF. This is a special-purpose vehicle established by the EU's 27 member states at the onset of the Greek crisis in

May 2010. The idea was to have a fund to help preserve financial stability in Europe by providing financial assistance to eurozone states in difficulty. Its first client was Greece, and it has been working on a facility for Portugal. Toward the end of 2010, Ireland reluctantly came knocking. But the fund is simply not big enough to bail out Spain.

Spain has pledged to reduce its deficit to 6 percent of GDP in 2011, and the bond market is keeping a vigilant eye on the country's progress toward that goal. Indeed, some statistics released by the government in late 2010 showed that the deficit had declined 42 percent through August 2010.[14] This was attributed to taxes that were over 30 percent higher year over year plus an increase in the value-added tax (VAT). The news calmed the bond markets a bit, but some analysts questioned the validity of the government statistics. Spain is a nation where the regional governments have a high degree of power and autonomy. Spain's announced deficit reduction referred to the central government and conveniently excluded budgets of the municipalities, which are not part of the central government's figures. Indeed, Spain's regional governments are increasing their deficits, not reducing them. Yet the goal remains a national deficit of 6 percent of GDP for 2011, a goal that few outside the central government believe possible. In September 2010, Prime Minister Jose Luis Zapatero, in an interview in the *Wall Street Journal,* declared, "It's evident that the Spanish Government has taken decisions that, in our opinion, are essential to confront the challenges that the Spanish economy faces during the crisis."[15]

Huh? Maybe the problems are being confronted, but nothing in the data suggests that they are being confronted successfully. The measures taken by the Spanish government resulted in the government's lowering its growth projections for 2011 from 1.8 percent to 1.3 percent.[16] However, many economists warned that Spain may incur *negative* growth after the austerity measures, including a rise in the VAT, start to work their way through the system.

As bad as the economic statistics are, we are dealing not only with numbers but also with people in a potentially fragile and explosive environment. In late 2010, Spain's unemployment rate topped 20 percent, the highest in Europe. Figure 2.3 shows the trend in Spain's

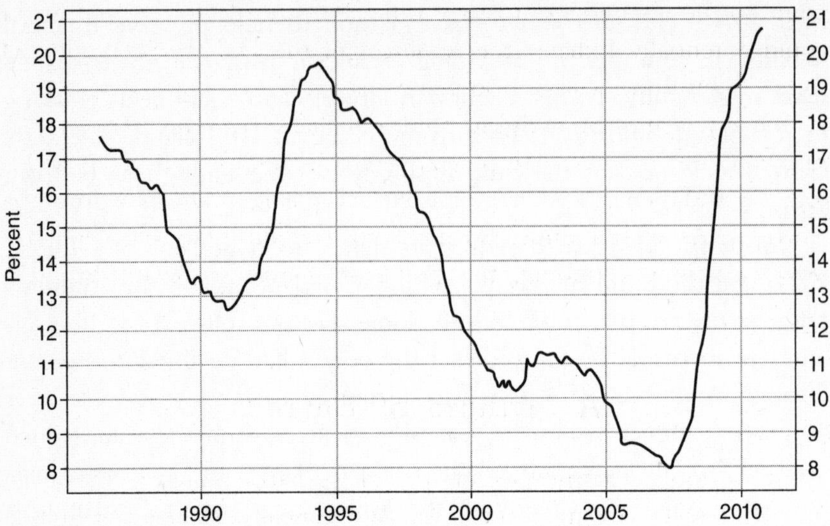

Figure 2.3 Spain's Unemployment Rate
SOURCE: Eurostat.

unemployment rate from the beginning of the crisis in early 2008 to late 2010. To call the trend alarming is an understatement. Moreover, Spain has strong labor unions, which consider their cradle-to-grave social benefits to be birthrights. Attempts to take away more of these benefits as part of the austerity program will be met with stiff resistance, or worse.

A Spanish default on its debt must be considered likely. Here is the situation that nation faces: Spain has close to 116 billion euros of loans coming due in 2011. It has no chance of paying them back, so it must refinance. We can't predict whether the markets will be receptive to continued massive borrowing by Spain, but this much is clear. We are as certain as we can be that the interest cost of any future Spanish borrowing will be considerably higher than the rates Spain paid in late 2010. In September 2010, Spain sold €2.7 billion of 10-year bonds at a very attractive rate (for the borrower, Spain) of 4.14 percent.[17] Rates for future borrowings are likely to be higher, and perhaps much higher. It is arguable that when Spain needs to refinance its huge debt in 2011, it will be either unable to do so, or able to but at rates so high as to be untenable. Will the IMF and European come to the rescue? Spain is five times the size of Greece, and Spain could potentially Exhaust the resources of the IMF/EFSF if allowed to, a doubtful proposition. So Spain may well be on its own.

Finally, it may be useful to point out that 2012 is an election year in Spain, and if Prime Minister Zapatero is interested in keeping his job, he had better find a politically acceptable solution before the elections. As we continue down the road of unsustainable debt in a slowly growing economy, this points to a Spanish default in 2011 or 2012.

A Plethora of Defaults

We have looked at the possible default scenarios in three European nations, Greece, Ireland, and Spain. We conclude that the default of all three will likely occur in late 2011 or sometime in 2012. Although we believe that Greece will be the first to default, circumstances may lead to the earlier default of one of the others or even one of the remaining countries in economic difficult like Portugal. Keep in mind that a default of one or several of these countries will not be taken in isolation. A coordinated strategy will surely be developed by the leadership of the European Union, especially since a wave of defaults will put the major European banks in peril, an event we will examine next.

How might this unfold? We've taken the liberty of fantasizing the beginning of the crisis as it plays out in this fictional account from the headquarters of the European Central Bank in Frankfurt.

The Crisis Begins—A Fable

ECB President Jean-Emile de Becque paced his office and gazed out at the magnificent 14th-century St. Bartholomeus' Cathedral towering over the old city of Frankfurt. It was a rare clear day in the German capital of finance, the appropriate headquarters for the European Central Bank, over which de Becque presided. Of course, Germany was not France, and Frankfurt was not Paris, where de Becque usually spent his weekends. But this particular Friday, he would not be going home to Paris. On this bright day, a monumental financial crisis was brewing and the future of Europe and the monetary union that had consumed the major part of de Becque's professional life hung in the balance.

Gerhard Stueffel, de Becque's brilliant aide for the past four years, barged into his office without knocking, as was his custom. Stueffel spoke in fluent French.

"We secured the Chateau du Lac at Genval les Eaux. It's just outside Brussels. I have been assured of the utmost discretion and full secrecy," Stueffel snapped.

De Becque nodded. He knew the place, an elegant castle on a lake with lovely rooms, manicured gardens, and a particularly talented chef. But this time, none of the guests would be there for the cuisine, the fresh air, or any of the other coveted amenities.

"How many of the ministers are coming?" De Becque asked.

"Fourteen of the sixteen," Stueffel replied. "The Estonian minister is on a yacht and can't get off. The Dutchman's daughter is getting married and crisis or no crisis, he isn't missing it."

Earlier in the day, de Becque took a call on a scrambled line from the finance minister of Greece. Interest rates on Greek sovereign debt had soared to 17 percent and if the subject of the call was supposed to be a secret, the market seemed to know all about it. There were no quotes on credit default swaps for Greece anymore; the country's debt was for all practical purposes uninsurable.

The Greek minister informed the president of the European Central Bank that Greece had a 75 million euro maturity on its sovereign bonds coming up the following Tuesday, and they were not going to be able to make the payment. "Could it be refinanced?" De Becque asked. "No." The rates were already ridiculous. The markets assumed that a default was inevitable. De Becque sighed audibly into the phone.

"Monsieur de Becque?" the nervous voice from Athens asked, "can we count on another round of aid from the EU and the IMF?"

"I'll let you know," de Becque said somberly. They exchanged a few more words and the conversation was over, leaving de Becque in silence, save for the sound of his heavy breathing and the dull pounding in his chest.

De Becque mulled his options. Over the past three years, Greek debt had ballooned to over 300 billion euros, representing a staggering 160 percent of the country's gross domestic product. Back in May 2010, the EU and the

IMF came to Greece's rescue with a combined 750 billion euro package, enough to establish the Union's seriousness in defending the euro. The crisis calmed down almost immediately when Greece was left no choice but to agree to a punishing set of austerity measures, raising the retirement age, reducing government salaries, higher taxes, and the list went on. In addition, Greek officials pledged to reduce the budget deficit from 14 percent of GDP to 3 percent as required by the rules of the European Union.

De Becque smiled. Even a first-year economics student knew that the imposition of these measures would result in a drastic slowdown of the economy. Yet in order to meet the pledge of reducing the deficit, the country's economy would have to grow as never before! An impossible task. Yes, we asked the impossible. And now the phone is ringing again. Can we blame them?

As he paced his large office in silence, de Becque cobbled in his mind the type of rescue that he might propose to his colleagues from the 16 member nations (or in this case, from the 14 who were coming) who would attend his emergency weekend meeting in that little castle outside of Brussels. A Greek default would be chaotic and must be avoided. So it would be avoided.

At least, that's what de Becque thought until the phone rang again.

Stueffel boomed into the room, a look of Teutonic panic in his eyes. He whispered ominously: "Monsieur de Becque, the prime minister of Ireland is on the line."

Chapter 3

The Miserable State of the States

More than a decade of well-intentioned but hideous policymaking has brought us to the current predicament, which will culminate in the worst economic crisis in U.S. history. Much of the focus for these mistakes is on Washington, and deservedly so. Receiving far less attention on the topic of inflation is the role the states have played.

What makes inflation especially problematic is that it is an economic phenomenon with many causes and only a few solutions, none of them pleasant. It will take us the course of this entire book to diagnose all of the circumstances that have led us to this dreadful point, with Washington bearing much of the blame. But state and local governments have been every bit as much the villain in this debt and deficit drama. Federal policy makers baited the hook with low interest rates and easy access to credit and capital, and governments from Pennsylvania to California, from Michigan to Texas, bit and bit hard. Profligate spending on pork-barrel projects and the ever-swelling public payroll—all on the taxpayer dime and with the bills to be paid by generations to come—have played just as important a role in the current crisis as all of the shenanigans with Fannie Mae and Freddie

Mac and mortgage-backed securities and the too-big-too-fail institutions that sapped the life from the U.S. economy.

While the problems have festered for many years, 2010 was the year the chickens came home to roost. As the year was coming to a close, states grappled with a seemingly insurmountable challenge of closing $125 billion in budget deficits, a number expected to swell to $140 billion by 2012, according to the Center on Budget and Policy Priorities.[1] Of this total, dwindling federal help in the form of the Recovery Act will come to only $6 billion, a far cry from what will be needed to help the states out of their collective mess. Public payrolls have been slashed and entitlement programs gutted. Yet for all their labors, governors, state legislators, and municipal officials remain burdened by a problem that will only make the global debt and deficit calamity worse.

Solutions to this odious set of problems indeed will be hard to devise and even harder to implement. A toxic recipe of reckless fiscal and monetary policy, promulgated at all levels with no political or governmental bounds, has coalesced to form a cake that will taste bitter to most Americans. The rush of money supply to bail out Wall Street, combined with stunning levels of debt, will make these times feel more like the dour days of the late 1970s and early 1980s rather than the march into the new frontier that many of us had envisioned.

Much of the focus in the press, in academe, and in high-minded and low-minded political debates has been on the impact Washington's recklessness has had on the financial mess. And make no mistake, that's a good place to start. Had it not been for years of low-interest-rate, easy-lending policies, and blissful ignorance of the vast bubble forming in real estate, we likely would not be in this predicament. But the debate over what will cause the looming crash would be woefully incomplete without a close examination of the role that state governments played in a massive overflow of deficit spending that will drive up interest rates and inflation and make it progressively difficult to stanch the bleeding in employment. While we all watched in amazement as the federal government piled up a nearly $14 trillion debt and a $13 trillion budget deficit, states big and small were running up their own tabs. They flooded $2.8 trillion into the municipal bond market to fund all types of folly without the means to cover their debts, and now the tab is coming due.[2]

Harried in Harrisburg

Consider first the case of Harrisburg, Pennsylvania. While Governor Arnold Schwarzenegger and the fiscal miseries of California garnered all the headlines, Harrisburg's less-publicized case stood as a shocking example of how good governments go bad when they run up hundreds of billions in debt as just the normal cost of doing business. As this book was being written, Harrisburg had been placed under the auspices of Pennsylvania's Act 47 to address the gruesome debt service payments to finance misguided public works spending. Wrap your brain around that concept: A capital city in the United States of America's sixth-largest state population-wise had to contemplate restructuring (read *defaulting on*) its debt, and would have defaulted had the state government not stepped in. This is in a country where no investment is considered safer than that which is backed by the full faith and credit of the government.

How did Harrisburg get to such an awful place? A slew of relevant and tangential issues will bring anyone, be it a corporation, individual, or government entity, to bankruptcy, but the most common are loss of income and excessive debt. Harrisburg had both, though the latter easily outpaced the former in accounting for why a city just a few miles away from where Abraham Lincoln delivered the Gettysburg Address—which extolled the virtues of personal sacrifice and compassion—could be on the verge of becoming insolvent.

For Harrisburg, the problem traced primarily to a public works project that generated far too much debt and far too little revenue. (Dubious public works projects have been at the center of numerous cases of governmental financial woes for centuries, dating all the way back to the Holy Roman Empire, a concept we will explore in greater depth in the next chapter.) The city in 2003 borrowed $125 million to upgrade and retrofit its incinerator, an endeavor-turned-fiasco that the city thought surely would generate income. It took five years for the incinerator to reopen, and by then the city was awash in debt service payments it couldn't make on its $288 million debt load, exacerbated when city officials neglected to include a performance bond with the original debt issuance.[3] On May 1, 2010, the city missed a $452,282 loan payment related to the incinerator, and a true crisis was born.[4]

Talk about arrogance. Despite plenty of warning that the incinerator project was doomed for white-elephant land, the city pursued the project fecklessly and without regard to any of the general intellectual questioning and investigation that one might hope to expect from those entrusted with making such course-charting decisions. Harrisburg brought in a team of lawyers, accountants, and advisors who bestowed upon the city's leaders all the confirmation bias they would ever want and then some. Inexperienced firms were hired. Fees were paid for work poorly done. Loans were taken on disastrous terms. "Officials were aided, or rather misled, by the advice of numerous attorneys, bankers and engineers apparently far more interested in collecting handsome fees than they were in protecting the interests of taxpayers," wrote the *Harrisburg Patriot-News* editorial board in a scathing April 12, 2010, critique of the project. "As a result, there is a deep distrust of the fundamental institutions that created this fiasco."[5]

Pennsylvania, despite its bare-knuckles reputation in politics and its rugged blue-collar background, loves debt. The state's total debt was a whopping $137 billion for 2010, and the load will increase to $159 billion when 2012 hits and the greater global financial crisis looms.[6] The state also was on the hook for $3 billion it borrowed from the federal government to pay for unemployment claims. That in itself was a debt burden of $238.69 for each Keystone State resident. So you see where we're going with this: The governmental apple doesn't fall far from the debt tree. Harrisburg played follow the leader for its debt-loving governmental brethren just down Market Street a ways at the state Capitol. Pennsylvania, in turn, has followed the lead of its debt-addicted mother ship in Washington. As *The Sopranos'* Paulie Walnuts once so elegantly stated, "And on and on it goes, this thing of ours."

We'll have more on the Sopranos' own New Jersey a little later in this chapter when we talk about one of a handful of states where leaders actually are doing something to try to break the debt cycle and move responsibly into the future.

Gambling on Pennsylvania

Harrisburg is hardly the only city in the great Commonwealth of Pennsylvania to suffer from debts and deficits. Just a little ways east on Interstate 78, the city of Allentown—once immortalized in song by Billy Joel as a forlorn example of American decay—also has faced extreme budgetary hard times, caused in large part by an unfunded liability in its pension fund and not helped by generations of reckless borrowing practices. Luckily, though, for Allentown and its sister city, Bethlehem, the Lehigh Valley has a plan: to get lucky, literally. Both communities, beset by crushing budget pressures that they can no longer get out from under independently, are depending on scads of cash coming from the Las Vegas Sands casino, which opened in Bethlehem in 2009. The casino, a hulking monster of a building constructed entirely without character or nuance on the old Bethlehem Steel property, has nonetheless been a cash cow for the two communities, which split its revenue. Other municipalities across the Commonwealth are playing the same game, hoping they'll draw blackjack the hard way and find a way to paper over their troubles. The Bethlehem casino was among the biggest draws of the 10 gambling halls opened in the state after the Legislature legalized gambling. The Sands was bringing in about $5 million a week in revenue in late 2010, outpacing others in the Philadelphia and Pocono Mountain areas. It's raining gambling money in Pennsylvania and everyone, it seems, is getting wet, especially the Keystone State's beleaguered residents, who continue to get soaked with taxes despite the strong revenue stream gambling has provided. For now, though, the crisis has been averted in these two struggling cities as well as this flailing blue-collar state.

Word of Pennsylvania's foray into gambling has spread among other debt-plagued states. Illinois was moving toward an aggressive gambling expansion itself and planning to borrow $4 billion for pension payments. Of course, that would be in addition to the 67 percent increase in the state income tax, and a 45 percent hike in corporate taxes for 2011 that the state enacted in an effort, along with its possible gaming foray, to close a $13 billion budget gap. And this, ladies and gentlemen, is what passes for fiscal management in our nation's cities and states: Gambling on gambling to help pay the bills.

The troubling reality, though, is that the problems of debt and deficits elsewhere will not go away so easily. Thirty-two states had run up a tab approaching $40 billion in borrowing to pay unemployment claims alone. Why? Because they've simply run out of their own money to pay off the burgeoning unemployment claims that the jobless recovery has brought. And like the shylocks who populate the Bada Bing strip club on *The Sopranos,* Washington is no soft touch as a creditor. Congress was threatening that if the unemployment debts weren't paid, the states were going to lose an important federal tax credit. As many as 25 of the 32 states were expected to be unable to pay their debt, and congressional leaders are unlikely to extend the tax credit.

We wonder just how many signals it will take to show that when the current conditions have presented themselves before, inflation always has followed. This is no more apparent than it is with the state of the states. The last time states faced such an onerous debt burden was in the severe inflationary times of 1983, when the total unemployment debt, adjusted for current dollars, was about $28 billion.[7] That's nearly one-third less than the current situation, and back then the inflation rate had just crested from the double-digit nightmares of the late 1970s and early 1980s. Congress in those days was a good deal more sympathetic to the plight of the states and enacted a series of measures that not only alleviated the unemployment debt burden but also planted the seeds for the robust recovery that would make the 1980s a comparative golden era of fiscal policy. The government increased an unemployment tax for businesses (as a stop-gap measure to alleviate the debt burden) and provided tax incentives for state governments that showed willingness to install austerity measures.

But those policies alone came well short of sealing the gap and, as we shall see later, the feds can do only so much to help the states.

It instead was the subsequent moves toward reducing the tax burden across the board, spurring a broad economic recovery, that helped pay down all that debt. It is hard to imagine the current Congress being brave enough to make the tough decisions its predecessors did a generation ago, and harder still to imagine a robust recovery that will help generate the revenue that will wipe out all that choking debt on states' books.

Certain economic truisms also will help trigger the crisis we are forecasting. One of the cornerstones is that higher budget deficits produce higher debts, which produce higher interest rates, which produce inflation. This symbiotic relationship is important to restate here because one of the mantras in 2010 among smart and learned economists was that the far greater risk to American economic security will come from deflation. In making their case, they cite Japan's lost decade in the 1990s, from which it has yet to recover. Japan's GDP growth rate went from 3.324 percent in 1991 to −0.141 percent in 1999. In the following decade growth never exceeded 2.744 percent and was −5.369 percent in 2009, according to the International Monetary Fund. There are those who see similarity, reasoning that because both crises were triggered by a real estate bubble and Japan then suffered deflation, then—voila!—that clearly means the present danger to the United States is not inflationary. Such nonsense is hard to fathom, especially considering that it comes from fairly reasonable sources, including Federal Reserve governors, who ought to know better. Consider only a few of the differences to know that Japan is clearly not where we are heading:

When the subprime mortgage crisis began to intensify in 2007, the Federal Reserve reacted quickly—not as quickly as some would have preferred—but nonetheless in a rapid and unprecedented manner (indeed, we say, so quickly as to be reckless). Whereas the Bank of Japan took 17 months to attack its financial crisis, the Fed began its easing program in far shorter time once the gravity of the crisis became clear. Starting August 17, the Fed cut its key lending rate three times in 2007 and followed that up with seven more cuts in 2008. At the same time, the Fed opened up a can of alphabet soup in the form of programs to provide a stopgap in the financial system. The U.S. central bank pumped liquidity into the system as well as confidence that the government would step in to backstop any such further disturbances. Trouble is, all that liquidity and all that intervention, in addition to providing a Band-Aid on what ails the U.S. financial system, also planted the seeds for the financial crisis yet to come as crippling inflation looms large in the background.

Waiting for the Tax Man

The concept of an inflation recession is something we'll explore a little later, but a decade of monetary and fiscal mismanagement is pushing us precisely in that direction. The cost to eat, the cost to borrow, the cost to drive your car—they all will increase dramatically as the looming crash reverberates while all the time actual economic growth will be hampered. Many experts link economic growth measures such as gross domestic product to the possibility of inflation, and it is a fatal mistake. For while we thoroughly agree with the experts at Pacific Investment Management Company, aka PIMCO, that the "new normal" is likely to entail several years of substandard growth, we wholly reject any argument that this minimizes the possibility of inflation. Rather, the recession-like mode of growth the United States is likely to experience will only exacerbate the pain that will be felt once the debt begins impacting interest rates and the growth of emerging market economies pushes commodity prices ever higher despite anemic U.S. growth in wages. Indeed, PIMCO's Bill Gross and others at the world's leading bond fund warned in early 2011 that inflation was becoming a much bigger danger.

This slow growth will precipitate another major contributor to the tumult ahead: tax increases that will be implemented to pay off the states' debt tab. Inflation, of course, is its own tax. As the government prints more and more money to monetize its debt, it cheapens the value of the currency and more cash is required for buying the same amount of goods. Responsible pro-growth governments know that the best way to stabilize the economy in such an environment is to lighten the tax burden. But in the present political climate, tax cuts, especially those that benefit the greatest wealth-producers in society, are treated as anathema. Demonizing the wealthy is No. 1 on the hit parade of populist panderers, who will try to achieve politically what they cannot economically. It's an easy game to play pin-the-tail-on-the-rich-guy, but it does little to address the underlying causes of economic malaise.

As Representative Ron Paul, the firebrand Texas Republican, once wrote of the zeal to tax the rich:

> *[A]ll we hear is that tax cuts for the rich are the source of every economic ill in the country. Anyone truly concerned about the middle class suffering from falling real wages, under-employment, a rising cost of living, and a decreasing standard of living should pay a lot more attention to monetary policy. Federal spending, deficits, and Federal Reserve mischief hurt the poor while transferring wealth to the already rich. This is the real problem, and raising taxes on those who produce wealth will only make conditions worse.*[8]

That is deftly stated, but alas we live in times where high taxes are the lifeblood of governments big and small, and the prevailing approach is that the bigger the wealth-creator the better when it comes to deciding who to sock with the big-ticket tax rates. Wealth transfer is being accomplished at breakneck speed, except it's about to be low- and middle-income earners who will feel the greatest bite.

As 2010 got under way, just two states—Montana and North Dakota—were not running budget deficits. A few states got the message during the year, closing their shortfalls with brave austerity measures aimed at taking a hunk out of the places that should have been cut long ago—silly public works projects, overfed education budgets, and the perks and privileges that were driving state governments into oblivion. But much more trouble remained on the horizon evidenced by the virulent protests in Wisconsin.

For 2011, the projected total budget gap for all 50 states was $122 billion, which came to nearly one-fifth of the total state budgets.[9] Research from the Center on Budget and Policy Priorities showed that the shortfall likely would increase to $140 billion by the time all was said and done, and it could be worse depending on how much largesse Congress is willing to extend in the form of subsidies to the states that have been running up these enormous deficits. These budget deficits have been triggering a wave of borrowing by states that no longer can count on revenue and organic economic growth to help pay their bills. For their borrowing, they will pay higher interest rates, which will help drive the inflationary spiral. There simply is no other possible outcome. No wonder, then, that in January 2011, talk in Washington began to turn to letting states go bankrupt and developing some type of mechanism to bring them back to solvency, along the lines of the Wall Street bailouts.

Remember: All states except Vermont are required to have balanced budgets. That means the missing revenue will have to come from somewhere, and there are only two alternatives in the current political climate. Either the states will add to their massive debt burdens, or like Illinois they will find new and exciting ways to soak you, the taxpayer, with the bill—or, in the most likely scenario, a nightmarish combination of both evils.

Taxes, Taxes, Everywhere

These taxes will come from a variety of sources, many of which will be inspired by our legislators' never-sated desire for more and more social engineering: They'll tax your gas because you shouldn't be driving so much; they'll tax your beer because you shouldn't be drinking so much; they'll tax your candy because you shouldn't be eating so much. Texas, Pennsylvania, and Georgia weighed "pole taxes," which would be collected from patrons of strip clubs. Nevada is looking at raising its prostitution taxes. New York and several other states have increased their candy and soda taxes, though voters in Washington state rightly rejected such a proposal as hideously regressive and ineffectual. California is expected to keep pressing for marijuana legalization as it ponders all the additional tax revenue pot-smokers can create, despite an electoral setback in 2010. And a whole host of states—we already mentioned Pennsylvania and Illinois and their moves in this direction—are examining the ways they can use legalized gambling to goose their state kitties. Now we can all debate the morality or lack thereof regarding the preceding activities, but one point remains clear: States don't much care about your vices, so long as they're getting a cut.

Within this vicious cycle is a negative feedback loop of the highest degree. The economic uncertainty, hanging like a supersonic jet in search of a landing strip, keeps businesses from hiring new workers and ensures at best a jobless recovery. That in turn depresses income levels, which depresses tax receipts and sends governments looking for ways to make up the shortfalls. With little political appetite for austerity, too many are turning either to borrowing or taxation. That in turn creates economic uncertainty and generates the negative feedback loop, which will spin and spin until the impending crash becomes a crushing reality.

So, is there any hope of saving our economy? Yes, there is hope. As faint as it is, there is reason to believe that some people get it, that some policy makers willing to risk their political futures are trying desperately to blaze a path toward fiscal responsibility. Should they succeed, they could become the template for a nation. Should they fail, it will be primarily because of the onus of a federal government run amok, with debts and deficit spending and massive entitlement programs that will add hundreds of billions to the federal burden. To show we are not all doom and gloom, to demonstrate that we do believe there is reason yet that America can emerge from the shadows of this dark era, we close this chapter by focusing on a few of the efforts from leaders who want to avoid the economic crash.

Despite all its bad press, California actually has been trying to close its budget gap through progressive measures. Governor Arnold Schwarzenegger, in the waning days of his tumultuous term, took a hard line against recalcitrant unions that have long dictated their own terms. He instituted spending and pay cuts that helped the state's almost unmanageable financial mess. Though predictions abound that the California has merely forestalled its own crash until perhaps 2014, the state was making progress. Rising pension and unemployment costs will be the next hurdle for California to cross, and things will get very interesting if Schwarzenegger's successor, Jerry Brown, lacks the temerity to take on the root of the problem.

But investors were growing impatient with California's efforts to get its house in order, threatening the stutter-step measures of progress the state had been making.

The possibility of a failed bond auction remains America's greatest economic nightmare and would be the trigger for the economic forecast made in this book. The day when investors tire of the debts and deficits on the U.S. balance sheet, along with the aggressive devaluation of the dollar, is the day when the great reckoning comes. As we will explain later in fuller detail, a failed Treasury auction would send interest rates soaring and trigger a stock market collapse of a magnitude not seen before on these shores. We raise this point now because late in 2010 California provided an early glimpse of investor attitudes toward government fiscal management.

With bills piling up and the overtaxed Golden State struggling to make ends meet, the state scheduled a $10 billion bond sale to help plug a budget shortfall expected to reach $25 billion by the end of the fiscal year in June 2012. The auction was for the sale of what is known in municipal accounting offices as a TRAN—a tax and revenue anticipation note. Governments large and small issue these bonds at generally low rates—usually around 1 percent—because they are historically safe bets and are particularly attractive to large institutional investors such as the ones that control endowments and pension funds. As the name implies, the bonds are short term and issued against future receipts the government in question will get from taxes, fees, and investments. They're not tied to the success of a public works project or anything else. Institutional investors looking for extreme safety usually snap up TRAN without hesitation. But in California's case, things went awry.

Just 60 percent of the securities were sold in the first day, necessitating a rare extension of the auction for what otherwise is an easy sell. If this occurred at the federal level, news outlets would be in full throat about a "failed auction," but in California's case the reaction wasn't quite as drastic. *Business Insider* ran a headline and a 16-part online slideshow titled "Why California is the Next Greece," but Michael Pietronico, CEO at Miller Tabak Asset Management, insisted to the *Wall Street Journal* that "This is not a sign that California is having problems selling its debt in our view."[10] Still, there was only so much one could do to avoid the implications. "California's timing unfortunately couldn't be worse," Deutsche Bank Private Wealth's Gary Pollack told the *Journal*.[11]

Indeed, the weak auction was noticed elsewhere, causing $700 billion in government bond sales to be taken off the table, while investors started yanking money out of municipal bond exchange-traded funds and into emerging market and gold funds. For much of the capital market rally in 2009 and 2010, municipal bonds were seen as the fair-haired child of the debt markets, but the worm was clearly beginning to turn.

It would be unfair to say that the states collectively are not trying to solve the problem, though they surely are quite late to the party. States cut nearly half a million jobs between 2009 and 2011—a sliver of the total public payroll, to be sure, but a start. And while the federal government was running up its expenses with hundreds of billions in stimulus and bailout money that totaled an average 18 percent annual spending increase since the start of the recession, the states were cutting spending by 2 percent. Local governments, meanwhile, furloughed 234,000 workers during the same period, which marks a 1.7 percent cut.

Near the end of 2010, Pennsylvania's Legislature approved a measure that would let workers choose to pay more toward pensions or to reduce benefits. The state also raised the retirement age for new workers. Minnesota gave outgoing Gov. Tim Pawlenty a going-away gift by approving spending cuts without raising taxes, eliminating a $3 billion budget deficit while allowing the governor to move low-income residents out of the state-funded health plan and over to Medicaid, which is funded both by the state and federal governments. As many as 15 states raised sales or income taxes in 2009 or 2010—an ultimately foolhardy move, since tax increases most often end up in revenue decreases.

Governmental job cutting has been a pittance compared to the overall hole in which the states and localities find themselves. But at a time of the worst economic downturn since the Great Depression, overcoming the appetite for spending is a daunting task. Interestingly enough, the political ramifications are clear for cost-cutters. Governors in New Jersey, Minnesota, and Indiana have cut costs aggressively while maintaining huge popularity ratings. After the November election, New York's Andrew Cuomo was one of a dozen governors to vow not to raise taxes to address their serious budgetary issues.

That is all well and good, but the greater work lies ahead, providing the most severe test of political will in a generation. The double-dip recession of the early 1980s saw the municipal labor force shrink 3.8 percent,[12] a historical benchmark that shows how much needs to be done compared to what has been achieved so far at that level. The role of the federal government, meanwhile, will remain a hotly contested point. Should Washington intercede in a state's problems, or should it tend to its own business and let the heartland fend for itself? While the congressional left believes in the heavy-handed involvement of Uncle Sam, evidence mounts that Washington can do more harm than good when it tries to intervene.

The Federal Reserve Bank of Chicago compiled an important research paper that examined the effectiveness of what happens when the federal government offers "help" to states in recessionary troughs. The report examined recessions in 1975–78, 1980–83, 1990–91, in 2001 following the 9/11 terrorist attacks, and in the 2007 financial system collapse. As you might guess, the grades were hardly glowing for Washington's role. The Chicago Fed's evaluation found that Congress was generally tone-deaf to the *types* of problems being felt by the individual states, releasing money that was ill spent, ineffective, and further contributory toward the erosion of the federal fiscal base. Our favorite sentence in the seventeen-page report:

> *If states believe that the federal government will always intercede to provide countercyclical relief, they will have little incentive to develop their own budgetary strategies to address recessions.*[13]

This is the "moral hazard," most often applied recently to the government's willingness to save the faltering banks during the 2008–2009 financial crisis but strongly applicable to possible bailouts for the states.

Hope, New Jersey

All of which brings us to New Jersey, home of the aforementioned Paulie Walnuts and the rest of the Tony Soprano crew—but more importantly to Governor Chris Christie, the nation's front-line leader in state frugality and a beacon for those hoping the Crash of 2012 does not need to be a fait accompli.

Surely nothing is certain when it comes to politics and government. But if history is any guide and politicians still get style points for character and courage, the story of Christie's revamping of the way New Jersey does business will be one worth retelling when the next crisis hits. It will be the tale of how one man took office in a state famous for profligate spending and a suffocating tax structure and stood it on its head.

Christie entered as the Garden State's 55th governor in January 2010 with the state languishing under an $11 billion deficit crushing its $29.4 billion budget. The Republican had to pick up the pieces following four unremarkable years under the stewardship of former Goldman Sachs CEO Jon Corzine. Though the Democrat Corzine made some headway in cutting fat from the state budget, his time in Trenton was marked mostly by a series of unpopular tax hikes—in particular the sales tax and highway tolls—as well as scandals involving appointments and incidents in his personal life. State spending increased nearly 50 percent from 2002 to 2008, and local spending rose 69 percent from 2001.[14] Burdened by all that along with the bloated budget and a reputation as the most-taxed state in the country, voters decided they'd had enough. The electorate ushered Christie and his reform promises into office amid hopes that he could steer them out of their recession.

Like his predecessor, Christie made the education system his first target. New Jersey is legendary for subsidizing low-income school districts, shoveling out hundreds of millions in dollars for white-elephant schools and in padding payrolls with political appointees to a level few states can match. Christie first slashed $820 million in education aid and $445 million in aid to municipalities, much of which fed the more than 600 school districts across New Jersey, with the hope of getting school districts to consolidate and find ways to cut costs. Christie also slapped a 2 percent cap on the amount municipalities can raise property taxes and cut state aid to local governments.

It wasn't just what Christie was doing; it was how he was doing it. In a state long run by unions and corrupt government officials, the freshman governor took charge. Immediately after it passed his budget plan, he ordered the state Assembly back into action over the July 4, 2010, holiday and demanded it enact his property tax cap, which started at 2.5 percent but fell even further as Christie entrenched his position. All the while, he was forging bipartisan coalitions with the Trenton leadership—political qualities foreign to his bumbling counterpart across the Hudson River, then-New York Governor David Patterson. Christie's self-proclaimed "tool kit" to achieve fiscal stability was a risky but essential strategy toward solving New Jersey's problems. The tool kit consisted of 33 bills that included the property tax cap as well as a slew of other proposals that he said would signify that "we are now taking action to bring to an end the current property tax crisis and giving people real relief. After talking about the direction we need to move, we now need to get down to business and enact these reforms."[15] Yet the governor's political will faces tests probably he cannot even currently imagine over the coming years.

The success of Christie's or anyone else's plan, of course, is going to depend on a lot more than courage and hope. New Jersey, too, is home to a town called Hope, which sits in the hills of Warren County along the Delaware River. The state will need all the hope it can get.

Doomed to Repeat

The negative feedback loop as unemployment continues to hold back the economy will be a massive roadblock to any attempt at recovery, as will further policy mistakes in Washington. And rest assured there will be mistakes. Policy makers have been trying to stem inflation for as long as there have been economists to misdiagnose the problem and governments to misapply solutions. In fact, government blindness to the root causes of inflation, as we shall see, go back to the Roman Empire and continue to the present day, all leading on a collision course with economic calamity.

Chapter 4

Inflation, through the Years

Diocletian (A.D. 244–311) may not be one of history's better known leaders, but his efforts stand 1,700 years later as an important lesson both literal and allegorical about what happens when government becomes overzealous in its attempts to control the money supply and manipulate free-market efficiencies. Policy makers continue to make many of the same mistakes as this otherwise-competent emperor—and to equally disastrous results. His Edict on Maximum Prices, issued in 301, serves as the template for government-created inflation and one of the earliest examples of unheeded government mistakes on monetary policy. A well-intentioned but misguided effort, the edict fomented wild price deviations and economic unrest in the Roman Empire.

Born Gaius Aurelius Valerius Diocletianus, he rose to power upon the death of the emperor Carus, inheriting a slew of thorny problems: a tangled political structure, a government spending scads of money to expand its empire, and a middle class under intense pressure. The currency suffered severe debasement due to profligate welfare and public works programs, and the suffering public blamed the free markets and greedy businessmen for their plight. Amid the economic turmoil, government increased its intervention programs to try to quell the storm, with each effort at manipulation only making the problems worse.

Finding any of this familiar?

Enter Diocletian. A reasonably bright man despite his lack of pedigree—unlike many heirs to the throne, Diocletian came from humble origins—he thought he had the answer to Rome's problems, which were multitude. For centuries his predecessors had been propping up the grain market by buying corn and wheat in times of shortage and reselling it at discount prices. Over time, these discounts became freebies and soon created a welfare state, with little incentive for farmers to keep toiling in their fields while the government was rewarding idleness. Eventually the government discovered the problem with handing out free food, and Julius Caesar curbed the practice somewhat. But subsequent rulers, in an attempt to keep the economy moving, felt forced to devalue the Roman currency by cutting the gold and silver content of various coins, and the results were predictable—wildfire inflation throughout the kingdom. In Egypt, the price of wheat over a 250-year period skyrocketed from six drachmai to two million!

Diocletian would have attributed Roman inflation to greed from wealthy store owners and speculators, much like the latter are blamed for the market excesses of today. His detractors, conversely, would contend that the emperor himself caused all the problems with wanton empire-building, pork-barrel public works projects, and the massive expansion of government (Diocletian, in addition to being an inflationist, was also a bureaucrat). No matter. Historians affix the causes of inflation during Diocletian's time to a variety of factors, some of his making and some not. Indeed, Diocletian was saddled with legacy issues, but it was his foolhardy attempt to fix the economic inequities that put an economic asterisk next to an otherwise peaceful reign.

Faced with a vexing problem, Diocletian issued an edict that attempted to curb the ravages of inflation but actually led to a series of serious policy errors.

The Edict on Coinage, as it became known, was the first of his follies. The order halted the production of worthless gold and silver coins and mandated the manufacture of a new coin made of an even lower-grade metal, copper. This literal devaluation of the national currency, as expected, pushed prices sharply upward. But Diocletian soon learned that if he wanted to keep his own Era of Big Government running, currency devaluation would have to continue to be the order of the day. Thus came the second, and far more damaging, edict from Diocletian.

Issued near end of 301, the Edict on Maximum Prices was etched on public buildings throughout the kingdom. And give the emperor credit: The manifesto that accompanied the edict was a brilliant socio-economic treatise about the ravages of greed and, ultimately, its effect on the prices of goods. Even though Diocletian made clear that the "capital penalty" would apply to violators of the law, the brutality that would accompany violations was masked with a master stroke of rhetoric in which the emperor displayed compassion for the plight of the populace:

> *Some people always are eager to turn a profit even on blessings from the gods: they seize the abundance of general prosperity and strangle it. Or again they make much of a year's bad harvest and traffic by the operations of hucksters. Although they each wallow in the greatest riches, with which nations could have been satisfied, they chase after personal allowances and hunt down their chiseling percentages. On their greed, provincial citizens, the logic of our shared humanity urges us to set a limit.*[1]

And set a limit he did. Diocletian regulated wages and prices on a multitude of goods, ensuring both the temporary halt of inflation in the empire and general economic chaos. Diocletian's problem in part was that he ordered the mass minting of new coins at the same time that he was trying to control prices. Any first-year economics major can tell you what happens next: With all that coin in circulation and the government artificially holding prices down, it would only be a matter of time before the marketplace would erupt and either demand higher prices for goods or put a halt to unprofitable labors. Consequences would rain throughout the empire, especially hitting the poor laborers, whose wages were frozen. As all that money kept flowing into the economy, their paltry salaries became worth less and less.

The sum of the damages: By the time Diocletian's reign ended in 305 and he took the theretofore unprecedented step of abdicating instead of either dying in office or being ousted, the Edict on Maximum Prices had about as much heft as a jaywalking citation might today. Indeed, Rome's citizens knew the law was in effect, but they, like the citizens today who don't bother to go to the corner to cross the street, knew the possibility of prosecution was minimal.

The lesson of Diocletian holds significance today in part because it provides a philosophical warning on overreaching government programs while vividly displaying the practical dangers of trying to devalue your way out of a crisis. Diocletian wasn't stupid, nor are today's policy makers who think there won't be a price to pay when the bill comes due for all those dollars out there in circulation. President Barack Obama and Federal Reserve Chairman Ben Bernanke are both smart men who believe extreme circumstances necessitated extreme measures. Timothy Geithner and his predecessor, Henry Paulson, both recognized the dangers of devaluation, but made reasoned and considered decisions to take that risk. Even as this book was being written, there was nary an economist to be found talking about inflation. "Deflation is the primary risk" is their mantra, the emerging specter of Nassim Taleb's Black Swan be damned.

Inflation: Is It Bigger Than a Breadbox?

This is a good time, then, to consider just what *inflation* is. If you ask your neighbor to define inflation, he'll probably talk to you about soaring prices for gasoline, beer, and groceries. And while these are all perfectly valid descriptions of the *effects* of inflation, they don't really address the *causes*. It is well to remember that this is not a case of the chicken or the egg. The causal relation is clear. Inflation happens when too much money chases too few goods, and the result is a rise, sometimes dramatic, in the prices of goods we have to purchase in order to conduct our daily lives.

We like to present a definition of inflation from the brilliant economist and philosopher David Hume, who found it "self-evident" that prices and inflation depended entirely on the supply of goods compared to the supply of money. Hume said an increase in the amount of goods means "they become cheaper," while an increase in money supply means goods "rise in their value."

Hume (1711–1776) saw the danger that excessive money in the economic system posed and studied closely its effects. So if we are to continue our linear thinking through the discipline of epistemology, Hume's simple observations that the supply of money and the phenomenon of inflation are inextricably linked are essential to the conclusions of this book. Pump so much money into the economy that it outstrips an optimal level of goods, and you get inflation. Simple as that. The cumulative impacts of all the inflationary pressures at hand will be discussed in greater detail in the ensuing chapter, but it is important to keep Hume's gentle analysis in mind as we take a further trip through the annals of inflation history.

Let us flash forward now from the Roman Empire into pre-Nazi Germany and the unfortunate legacy of the Weimar Republic, one of history's most profound examples of runaway inflation and yet another cautionary tale from which modern-day policy makers could learn much.

War's Heavy Cost, Measured in Wheelbarrows

At the height of the Weimar Republic's absurd inflationary environment, an American tourist could visit Germany and get a trillion marks for the price of one dollar. The problem, of course, was that those trillion marks probably wouldn't buy you much more than a soda or maybe a newspaper, which would be proclaiming a steady stream of ugly news about post–World War I Germany and the onerous requirements it faced from the Treaty of Versailles. Ultimately, German citizens' outrage at their leaders' capitulation following the Great War would spark the rise of a megalomaniac named Adolf Hitler. But for now the nation was left to grapple with the 132 billion goldmark obligation it faced as the tab for losing the war.

At first, the Weimar policies were popular and the country thrived until the U.S. stock market collapsed in 1929. The concept of borrowing money from other nations—primarily the United States—seemed a reasonable way for the Germans to get out of hock as long as the economy continued to produce and the country adopted reasonable economic standards. But the rising deficits, worsening trade balance, and surging unemployment put the country at great risk.

Despite the pleadings of John Maynard Keynes, J. P. Morgan, and other great financial minds of the day for austerity, the Germans essentially were left helpless, unable to find a market for government bonds to help pay their debts and with global pressure building for reparations. With little appetite for belt-tightening, reining in speculators, or putting the clamps on reckless bankers, the government instead chose to print money—lots and lots of money. As German currency flooded the market, inflation went crazy. Stories of the German inflation contagion are legion and legendary. Prices doubled in a matter of hours. The saw about people taking wheelbarrows full of money to buy a loaf of bread was born. The German money printers had run amok, and consumers were paying an unfathomable price.

Germany's descent into hyperinflation occurred under circumstances that are all too familiar. The hubris of its government leaders had been the beginning and endpoint as they recklessly led the nation into a war it was sure it could not lose. They suspended redemption of its notes in gold, on the belief that once the Germans crushed their enemies there would be plenty of money to go around as the nation enjoyed its newfound world dominance. Of course, once things didn't go the Germans' way and the bills came due after World War I, there was so much money in circulation that the battlefield humiliation gave way to economic catastrophe.

It actually took a few years for inflation to catch on in Germany. True, the consumer price index growth of 140 percent in 1918 seems like a staggering figure. But compared to the rest of the war-ravaged world, it was pretty much in line. The reason again was not hard to figure out: Wartime conditions necessitated Draconian rationing, and there was little appetite for luxury goods. Rather than spend all those dollars that had been issued over the war years, the citizenry and the major financial institutions saved their cash, as at least some people in Germany were not as convinced as the warmongers that victory was certain. So while the war raged on and the printing presses churned out fresh marks, all that cash just kept piling up, waiting to be released into the money stream.

As the years rolled on and six million Germans lost their jobs, the Weimar Republic's instability accelerated. When the Republic fell in 1933, the unemployment rate was 30 percent and Germans welcomed the Keynesian economics and the military industrial complex that followed. This, also, did not work, but at least it gave Germans some solace in the run-up to World War II.

Now, one can debate the historical relevance of the Weimar Republic ad infinitum. The German economy then (and now) was far smaller than the U.S. economy, and the nation had been destroyed militarily, economically, and psychologically by a war that would be fought once again in just a few decades. But the larger point is this: The United States need not suffer peril on the scale that the German republic witnessed for massive inflation to take hold; it need not fall prey to a state of affairs in which its currency literally becomes worthless. What would have to happen is only a state of affairs in which the United States finds that its dollar is no longer the haven of international investors and financiers and loses its status as the world's reserve currency. Americans would need to see only that the Chinese and the Japanese no longer considered it prudent to lend Uncle Sam money for 10 years with the meager payback of 3 or 4 percent in interest. Combine that with the massive debt and deficit spending that has characterized all inflationary periods, add in the rise in interest rates sure to come when the Federal Reserve is forced to put $2 trillion in mortgage-backed securities into the market, and you suddenly have the perfect storm for the next wave of superinflation to hit the economy.

In short, it would barely even take one good round of Taleb's Black Swans to start circling to set off a crisis for the U.S. government as it monetizes a $1.5 trillion budget deficit when no one is there to buy its paper.

And so—the devastating crash would ensue.

Let us now flash ahead from the 1930s to a few decades down the road for yet another history lesson—again one that has been devoutly ignored by present-day policy makers—of what can happen when the unthinkable becomes thinkable.

Paul Volcker and Carter's Malaise Days

James Earl Carter was the toothy peanut farmer from Plains, Georgia, whose directive as president was to restore faith in the nation's badly broken political system and to steer the economy out of the stagflation that had bedeviled the nation throughout the mid-1970s. The much-maligned President Carter also had to deal with the sins of his predecessors. The destruction of the Bretton Woods system and the ending of the gold standard in 1971 changed global monetary policy in a way for which few governments were prepared, the United States among them. While long lines at gas stations and burgeoning prices at the supermarket and elsewhere are a Carter legacy, it should be remembered that seeds for this economic catastrophe were sown well before Carter left the Georgia governor's mansion for 1600 Pennsylvania Avenue. Yet he will be remembered for all that and more, after taking steps of his own that only made matters worse. His political mismanagement was duplicated by few others ever to hold the office—a failure to his liberal base for not devoting even more resources to the burgeoning ranks of the unemployed and the other special-interest groups that dominated the left, and a constant target for his enemies who considered him anti-business and unwilling to make the unpopular spending cuts that would be needed to rescue the nation from its crippling deficits.

When the dust finally cleared, the Carter Malaise Days made way for the challenge of the Reagan Revolution. By March 1980 interest rates were soaring along at a staggering 18 percent rate, inflation hit a peak of 14.76 percent, and the 10-year Treasury note was yielding a gaudy 12.75 percent.

Carter nonetheless had weathered a primary challenge from the left and its liberal lion Ted Kennedy, the venerable Massachusetts scion to the throne of Camelot. Meanwhile, former California governor and B movie actor Ronald Reagan waited in the wings. A *Time* magazine article from March 24, 1980, summed up the political situation, describing in frank detail how Carter fought a spectacularly futile battle against runaway inflation by concocting a hapless recipe of wage controls and taxes on gasoline and corporate profits:

Essentially, Carter is opting for more inflation now in the hope of less inflation later. . . . The biggest question of all is whether Carter's plans will have enough shock value to break the inflationary psychology that has gripped the nation. The most familiar manifestation of that psychology has been the compulsion of consumers to dip into savings or to borrow in order to buy before prices go higher. That action turns the expectation of more inflation into a self-fulfilling prophecy.[2]

The *Time* piece went on to discuss the role that raw fear played in the rabid growth of inflation. Business leaders and investors felt that the stock market—not gold—was the ultimate hedge against inflation and was vastly undervalued. The Dow Jones Industrial Average hit a paltry high of 904 the day before Valentine's Day, which was below its close at the same time in 1964, during the early days of the Johnson administration. (Investors these days shudder to contemplate a Standard & Poor's 500 at such an anemic level, let alone the Dow, which usually runs 10 or 11 times the S&P.) But now investors were losing their faith in the equity markets on the grounds that corporate profits couldn't be trusted as legitimate and sustainable in times of such debased currency. With fears that inflation could jump past 20 percent and make companies' nominal quarterly profits a bad joke, investors began pulling their money out of stocks, sending the Dow to a 16 percent tumble in the weeks after Carter announced his inflation-fighting strategy. Investors would soon find another inflation hedge—gold—as the best choice for asset allocation in the turbulent years ahead.

Before issuing an almost too-obvious warning about the historical parallels vis-à-vis corporate profits earned on the back of devalued currency backstopped by an overly generous Uncle Sam, we return to the *Time* essay, for it is both fascinating and instructive. The author notes the worry over how risky the bank business model is when it borrows over the short term at low rates and lends long at higher rates, then cites pervasive concern that with bank lending tightening up, some undercapitalized small banks and even some big corporations could go under. Said Don Jacobs, then dean of the Graduate School of Management at Northwestern University: "We are headed for a paralysis of the financial markets. We will see red ink throughout the financial industry. It could be a disaster. For the first time in my life I am really concerned."

As we know, borrowing short and lending long, described derisively in the magazine piece and the object of harsh words of admonishment from Dr. Jacobs, would before long become the lifeblood of the American financial system—before, during, and after the system's stunning collapse beginning in 2007. In the time of Jimmy Carter, the fear centered on the price banks would have to pay because of the threat that rising interest rates posed. And rise they did, as everybody knew they would. The reason why they knew it is that Carter did one thing right during his awkward stewardship of the American economy, and that was to appoint Paul Adolph Volcker to be Fed chairman. Volcker was among the few public servants with any clout who understood that unnatural currency devaluation was no way out of an economic crisis.

For those who don't remember Volcker's time helming the U.S. central bank, it is a history lesson in itself. Volcker was without peer in the Fed's history before or since in his willingness to stand up to political special interests, his determination to keep America and its currency strong, and his willingness to talk straight even to people who wanted to string him up in front of the Fed building, as almost happened when irate farmers drove their tractors down C Street NW in Washington, D.C., and blockaded the Eccles Building. In the present era as the Fed keeps its funds target rate near zero, it is almost unfathomable to remember the days when Volcker raised the rate to 20 percent in 1981 after it had averaged a comparatively paltry 11.9 percent just two years earlier. It is equally unfathomable to recognize that while Carter appointed Volcker in 1979, he was reappointed by Reagan four years later, even though it would be difficult to select two presidents who approached their jobs more differently than Carter and Reagan. While Volcker will be remembered unfavorably by some who recall his role in the Bretton Woods matter, it is he who deserves the most credit for tackling inflation down to 3.2 percent from its surreal 13.5 percent rate in two years. It was too late to rescue Carter's legacy, but the aggressive revaluing of American currency through higher interest rates and the advocacy of tighter monetary and fiscal policy helped pave the way for one of the greatest economic resurgences in American history. Sadly, Volcker stands in the shadows of the Obama administration as chairman of the Economic Recovery Advisory Board, but his tenure at the Fed serves as the template for modern monetary policy management.

It is important to note that many Americans thought Volcker was riding the country into the poorhouse when he began the series of reforms that would transform the economy. His congressional critics howled that Volcker's tightening of the money supply and policies that sent lending rates over 20 percent would break the backs of business and crush the spirits of beleaguered Americans who had, essentially, made their peace with inflation. Even as their money bought less and less and the absurd increases in wages could not keep pace with the rising prices of goods, they had acclimated themselves to the prevailing conditions, essentially learning to live with a system that was consuming wealth at breakneck pace. Undaunted, Volcker made a series of decisions that earned him the scorn of the American public and brought intense criticism from Washington legislators who had grown weary of their constituents' cries.

"We're destroying the American dream!" bellowed Rep. Henry B. Gonzalez, a Texas Democrat who joined a chorus of other House members who tore Volcker to shreds during a hearing in the summer of 1981. Indeed, it was no fun being Paul Volcker in 1981. Democrats were bitter toward him because they believed he had wrecked Jimmy Carter's chances for reelection in the 1980 race, and Republicans loathed him for turning public opinion quickly against Reagan after The Gipper took office. There were protests across the nation against the Fed's policies, and a security guard was all that stood between the 6-foot-7-inch "Tall Paul" Volcker and a deranged man who slipped into the Fed building armed with a sawed-off shotgun and a fake bomb. Yet after all the turmoil, protests, and handwringing, Volcker's legacy of political courage lives on.

In the foreword to Joseph B. Treaster's excellent *Paul Volcker: The Making of a Financial Legend*, former Securities and Exchange Commission Chairman Arthur Levitt Jr. writes:

Without Paul Volcker's toughness and guts, we may never have broken the grip of rising inflation and declining productivity that plagued the United

States during the 1970s. And we surely would not have been positioned to enjoy record economic growth in the 1990s. It would have been amazing to think in 1982, but now inflation barely registers as a concern in the United States. For that, Americans have to thank Paul Volcker.[3]

Americans could be forgiven for forgetting about inflation during the past decade, but that's a mindset not entirely justified by the facts. In fact, just a year after Levitt observed American apathy toward inflation, things changed considerably. Inflation was above 3 percent for less than half of 2004, with the yearly rate coming in at a very manageable 2.68 percent. However, it began creeping up in a very deliberate manner thereafter, hitting an apex of 5.60 percent in July 2008, as the worst of the financial crisis was about to hit. Table 4.1 compares the periods 1980–1989 and 2000–2009, providing a hint about where we're going.

Table 4.1 Inflation and Interest Rates

Year	Inflation Rate	10-Year Treasury Note
1980	13.58	11.43
1981	10.35	13.92
1982	6.16	13.01
1983	3.22	11.10
1984	4.30	12.46
1985	3.55	10.62
1986	1.91	7.67
1987	3.66	8.39
1988	4.08	8.85
1989	4.83	8.49
2000	3.38	6.03
2001	2.83	5.02
2002	1.59	4.61
2003	2.27	4.01
2004	2.68	4.27
2005	3.39	4.29
2006	3.24	4.80
2007	2.85	4.63
2008	3.85	3.66
2009	−0.34	3.26

Table 4.1 was included not only because the 10-year note is considered the benchmark by which investors judge the bond market, but also because the bond market is often looked to as a leading indicator for inflation. In fact, its behavior of the past 30 years shows that one can learn very little about the future path of inflation when watching bond yields. The best we might be able to say is that the bond market was a coincident indicator for inflation through the 1990s and has been myopic in its view over the past decade. The worst we can say is that the bond market couldn't have been more wrong during the 1980s, when Volcker's monetary policies were pummeling inflation and the 10-year note didn't fall below 10 percent until 1986—long after inflation had been obliterated.

It is our studied opinion, however, that the bond market would have begun assiduously pricing in inflation during 2010 had it not faced the exogenous effects of the European debt crisis coupled with volatile equity markets that necessitated a flight to safety. Bonds had been the beneficiary of an enormous bull market for the better part of two decades. Fixed-income investors benefited greatly from a low-interest-rate environment that took hold after the 1980s economic recovery, and flatlining stock prices also caused portfolios to hold a healthy complement of government debt. But nothing lasts forever, and bonds are only as good as the low interest rates that support them. For reasons that will be explored later in this book, the changing rate environment—which will surpass the Federal Reserve's ability to counteract—is ready to knock the bond market from its lofty perch.

Brother, Can You Spare a Billion Dollars?

So, is there no good news as we travel this inexorable path toward rampant inflation brought on by debts, deficits, and a reckless disregard for history? As a matter of fact, there is. The good news is that we are not now, nor shall we ever be, Zimbabwe.

The unfortunate republic on the southern edge of Africa has become synonymous with the absurd extremes of inflation. Two years ago, at the apex of Zimbabwean hyperinflation, a single egg was going for 50 billion Zimbabwean dollars, about the equivalent of 32 cents in U.S. currency. At a peak of 98 percent per day, Zimbabwe's hyperinflation is the second worst in world history, trailing only Hungary's, which in July 1946 saw daily inflation of 195 percent as prices doubled every 15.5 hours. Other examples of massive hyperinflation of the past 100 years include Yugoslavia 1994, 64.6 percent per day; Germany 1923 (the Weimar Republic), 21 percent per day; Greece 1944, 17.1 percent per day; and China 1949, 13.4 percent per day.[4]

Zimbabwe's problems stem from a long road of monetary mismanagement and severe currency debasements that ultimately took on a life of their own. In fact, the nation's stated inflation rate is only a guess at this point, with an exact figure on the unfathomable state of affairs impossible to pinpoint. Let's just say it's bad and leave it at that.

So we restate: The United States is not Zimbabwe. Our economy is too large, our manufacturing base too sturdy, our policy safeguards too strong to allow such absurdity to hit our economy. But, as we stated previously in this chapter, we need not find the extremes predicted by such harbingers of doom as Marc Faber, the infamous Dr. Doom and author of the *Gloom Boom & Doom* report, who as recently as March 2009 predicted, in an interview with Bloomberg, that Zimbabwean hyperinflation was on the horizon for the U.S. economy.[5] His reasoning? Fed Chairman Ben Bernanke would be reluctant to show Volckerian courage by hiking inflation rates. The thinking is that with investors still skittish over the state of the economy, the Fed will continue its "extremely low for an extended period of time" language until there are sure signs of economic stability. And with bond manager PIMCO predicting that the New Normal would consist of years of slow growth, Bernanke will be restrained from taking any significant measures on its funds rate and thus spook investors that growth will be stunted.

"I am 100 percent sure that the U.S. will go into hyperinflation," Faber said. "The problem with government debt growing so much is that when the time will come and the Fed should increase interest rates, they will be very reluctant to do so and so inflation will start to accelerate." The latter part of Faber's statement makes much more sense than the former, and that is not an insignificant thing. Again, this book makes no claims that the United States is headed toward Zimbabwe-like inflation. Let us simply state for now that inflation is coming, inflation will be pronounced, and this high level of inflation will be far greater than the consensus economists and all their failed models will show.

If one looks through the course of history, the only condition not currently present that usually accompanies inflation is wage pressure. But this too relies on conventional wisdom—all the same conventional wisdom that has been betraying us through time since the beginning of the financial markets. The fact is that excessive wage growth absolutely, positively *is not* a requirement for inflation. Diocletian, as we recall, froze wages and still had inflation. Like rising supermarket prices, wage increases are at best an effect of inflation, not a cause. What has caused inflation over time, and what will cause inflation this time, is what has always caused it—an increase in money supply beyond the economy's ability to absorb.

Consider that money supply is increasing, not decreasing, albeit at a modest pace (2 percent when this was being written). Even at that rate, the fact is that the economy is on an inflationary path, not a deflationary one. And with policy makers and more particularly economists blissfully ignorant of the path we are on, it is a dream scenario for contrarians and those who believe in Black Swans.

Michael Pento, senior economist at Euro Pacific Capital, has been a leading carrier of the inflation banner, warning anyone who will listen that American monetary policy has been leading the nation on an inexorable path to inflation. According to Pento:

- The national monetary base over the past 10 years has increased from $600 billion to $2 trillion.
- Gold—the ultimate inflation hedge—has swelled in price from $300 an ounce to more than $1,400 as of March 2011.
- The dollar has lost 30 percent of its value, and the national debt stands at more than $14 trillion.

With all of that U.S. paper out there, the last thing the government wants to do is decrease the money supply as it would drive up interest rates and increase the cost of financing the debt. "A reduction in the supply of money (deflation) would cause the cost of debt to rise. An increase in the purchasing power of money also means it is more difficult to acquire the new money needed to reduce debt levels," Pento wrote. "Conversely, increasing the supply of money (inflation) reduces the cost of debt. With these incentives firmly entrenched, the last thing Americans will have to 'worry' about is deflation."[6]

Taken together, the current conditions, combined with the policy mistakes the government has consistently made since the start of the financial crisis, as well as our willful ignorance of all the lessons history has tried to teach, leads to only one conclusion: The U.S. economy is headed for a period of massive inflation. The only question is how bad it will get.

Chapter 5

Europe on the Brink

We have discussed a scenario where the three most vulnerable countries—Greece, Ireland, and Spain—are almost certain to default in the not distant future. We are fairly certain that Greece will launch the downward spiral, but we are less certain that the scenario will play out with consecutive defaults or occur as part of a master plan to stave off the worst consequences of the impending economic collapse. Let's examine some of the possibilities of how this might play out.

Chapter 2 included a little fable of how the crisis might unfold, whereupon the president of the European Central Bank would call an emergency weekend meeting of all the finance ministers of the 16 eurozone countries. We believe that this is the most likely scenario. The leaders of the European Union would discuss what actions they might take to avert a crisis. The problem is that Greece will take the position that it cannot under any scenario find a path to repaying its outstanding debt; hence a default is inevitable. At this point, Ireland, Spain, and Portugal will likely claim that they too have no alternative but to restructure their debt. After an exhausting initial discussion, most of the participants will conclude that trying to solve the debt problem with more debt and more austerity is the road to ruin and likely civil unrest. What is needed is not another rescue package, but the realistic recognition that the existing debt simply cannot be repaid.

Once this gloomy assessment is recognized as the new reality, the next phase of discussions will ensue. Of course, this might take more than one meeting, but in these days of instantaneous communications, the secret of what is occurring will not last long. Markets will become increasingly skittish and volatility will spike.

The first and most urgent question is a simple one: Can the eurozone survive? The rich countries, led by France and Germany, will argue that the eurozone must survive as an entity and that a solution must be found within the context of the single currency. Others will claim that if the euro survives, the only solution for countries like Greece is a massive default. If they simply withdrew from the eurozone and readopted their former currency, Greece could devalue its drachma, effectively a restructuring without using the dreaded word.

Four Scenarios for Navigating an EU Crisis

Let's examine some of the possible scenarios the European Union might adopt to try to navigate through the crisis.

Scenario 1: Maintain the Euro and Allow Some Countries to Default

If Greece, Ireland, Spain, and Portugal default, it would certainly ruin their credit but would it affect their common currency? Arguably, it would not. After all, there have been defaults in bonds denominated in dollars and the fact that the bonds were dollar bonds did not impugn the value of the dollar as a reserve currency. In 2001 and 2002, Argentina defaulted on a series of bonds denominated in dollars and backed by the Argentinean state. The default didn't hurt the U.S. dollar. It certainly had an effect on the defaulting nation, though.

As you might expect, defaulting on sovereign debt is not something that the European Union tolerates for its member states. Indeed, to be part of the European Union nations must agree to a series of conditions. The one we have focused on the most is the requirement that member nations may not have a budget deficit that exceeds 3 percent of GDP. What all of the nations have in common is that every single one has violated that covenant. Ireland's budget deficit is *10 times* the permitted amount! What does that mean for the conditions of membership of the European Union?

The countries with an egregious amount of debt have pledged austerity measures to bring their deficits in line and, as a condition of compliance, the European Union has offered rescue packages to Greece and Ireland and is prepared to offer aid to other member countries in trouble. But as we have discussed, it is unrealistic to expect that these countries can grow their way out of their deficit problems through strict austerity programs. So we examine the path down which we are headed, and we see no good solutions.

Let's go back to the original question of what to do with a country that defaults. Kick it out of the union? Or just let it default and continue to use the common currency?

Scenario 2: Continue to Bail Out the Countries in Trouble

This is, of course, what happened in the case of Greece, followed by Ireland. But if Spain goes, game over. The country is too big to save. So we will not spend too much time on this option. As we said before, you cannot solve a debt problem by piling on more debt. Perhaps that might work in the short term, but it hasn't worked yet. More debt tends to make a debt problem worse. The logic is compelling.

Scenario 3: Create a Two-Tier Eurozone

Another idea bruited around the corridors of wealthier European states is a two-tier currency solution to the economic problems. The idea would be to create a "super-eurozone" consisting of France, Germany, Holland, Austria and Finland to start. In essence, the result would create a north/south divide with the rich countries nested in their own currency union and no longer saddled with the responsibility of bailing out weaker members. The have-not countries, like Greece, Spain, Portugal, and Ireland, would constitute the "poor cousin" currency union. The new eurozone, or super-eurozone, would have considerably higher value in international transactions than the old euro. Frankly, this plan seems born more out of frustration than logic. If you wonder how this might work, so do we.

Scenario 4: Shrink the Eurozone

The final option is to recognize that the eurozone simply embraced countries that were too dissimilar from the original senior members to allow the union to work. After all, was it really reasonable to assume that Estonia and Greece would live by the same economic rules as France and Germany? In the light of day a realization that the economic union was doomed from the start may well be recognized, albeit somewhat late. When the EU started using the euro and member countries abided by all the rules in early 2002, all the countries were on an upward economic trajectory, so compliance was relatively easy. After the worldwide financial crisis in 2008, the paths diverged and some countries fared far better than others. In 2010, Greece became the poster child for fiscal and economic mismanagement. Ireland and Spain followed suit, although their problems were more significantly rooted in the collapse of their real estate markets.

As a result, the most likely scenario is that the leaders of the EU will recognize that many of its member states do not have the ability to maintain the conditions of a common currency with some of their neighbors. Those countries that clearly cannot abide by the rules of the game will be let go. Goodbye Greece, Ireland, Spain, Portugal, and maybe even Italy. Ciao, bambini!

European Banks Begin to Tremble

When we discuss the possibility and even likelihood of a wave of sovereign credit defaults in Europe, we must immediately jump ahead to consider the consequences of these defaults. The first question is: Who holds the bonds that will default? Easy answer: The European banks hold the vast majority of these securities. Therefore, we must turn our attention to what might happen to these banks in the event of a default.

First, some recent history.

Back in spring 2010, when the fears of a Greek default surfaced and created havoc in the world's financial markets, attention immediately focused on the European banks that held most of the Greek sovereign debt. At the time, European banks and financial institutions held more than 130 billion euros of Greek, Portuguese, and Spanish debt. As a result, the European Union and the IMF jointly worked out an immediate rescue plan to allay fears in the markets. To show that they meant business, the partnership shocked the world's financial centers by announcing in May 2010 a 750 billion euro ($1 trillion) bailout fund.[1] The markets calmed almost immediately. This rescue package was on top of a 110 billion euro rescue fund for Greece alone, which was teetering on bankruptcy.

These measures would serve for the immediate problem, but European officials knew that they wouldn't be enough to stave off a long-term crisis. In the past, no one paid much attention to the sovereign debt held by the banks because these loans were considered riskless. After all, European countries don't go bankrupt, do they? The answer to that question was now on the table. Thanks to Greece, the game had changed. Questions would continue to be asked about the health of European banks, particularly in the event of another sovereign debt crisis down the road. As a result, a "stress test" was ordered to determine the health and risks of the 91 largest banks in Europe. As part of the test, banks were required to disclose the amount of European debt they held as of March 31, 2010.

The banks labored furiously to comply with the tests and when the results were released in late summer, they were surprisingly benign. Indeed, the Committee of European Banking Supervisors that conducted the tests revealed that only 7 of the 91 banks failed the test and would be required to raise additional capital in the event of a further crisis. It didn't take long for the financial press to dig into the commission's findings and find considerable fault with them. One paper noted that the stress test considered only the bonds that the banks were holding in their "trading books," shorter investments that must be valued at market prices.[2] It did not consider the much larger holdings in their banking book, since these are going to be held to maturity. Now the stress test was to look ahead two years, and since the banks weren't going to sell the bonds in their banking books, they assumed there was no likelihood of default over the next two years, especially since the EU and the IMF has so generously provided a 750-billion-euro bailout fund. Take a look at the size of what we're talking about. The amount of exposure of all the European banks to EU government debt in their trading book—which is all the test considered—was about 300 billion euros. The amount in the banking book, which the stress test ignored, was 1.3 trillion euros! The authors of the Organization for Economic Cooperation and Development paper determined, using the stress test's own worst-case-scenario, that the banks' total losses would be 165 billion euros, a much higher figure than the 26 billion euros the stress test reported.

Are you feeling comforted yet?

It gets worse. In many cases, banks didn't include in the stress test short positions in European sovereign debt, simply netting them out (or subtracting them) of their long positions, which had the effect of showing a smaller exposure. Some banks didn't reveal bonds held by their subsidiaries. For example, France's Credit Agricole didn't include the debt held by its insurance subsidiary. So, some economists compared the results of the stress test and the reported exposure of the banks to European debt and compared those figures to those compiled by the Bank for International Settlements (BIS). The stress test had reported that four French banks, representing about 80 percent of all the assets in French banks, held a total of 11.6 billion euros of Greek debt and 6.6 billion euros of Spanish debt. Compare that to the BIS data, which indicated that as of March 31, 2010, the French banks held not 11.6 billion euros, but 20 billion euros of Greek sovereign debt and not 6.6 billion euros, but 35 billion euros of Spanish government debt. This gets scary, doesn't it?

Bond traders and investors are not oblivious to these problems. For one, the bond credit rating agencies have all downgraded the debt securities of the troubled EU nations, but as we have all come to realize, the credit rating agencies remind us of the old saying about locking the barn doors after the cows have gone. By the time a credit gets downgraded, it is generally way too late for investors. The good news is that Spain and Greece have been able to borrow. The bad news is that they keep borrowing at higher rates reflecting the increased risk investors associate with their credits.

Staggering Losses

One point is clear. The European banks will not under any circumstances be able to withstand multiple defaults of European credits. Remember, European banks have a total exposure to European sovereign credits of 1.9 *trillion* euros, an unimaginable sum. Of course, not all of those credits will go bad. Germany and France are not about to default. But a default or restructuring of only the weakest of the nations in Europe would result in potential losses and write-downs of hundreds of millions of euros of sovereign debt, and the banks will simply be unable to support losses of that magnitude.

Clearly, we are not the only ones to realize this fact. The leadership of the European Union is well aware of the consequences of multiple defaults on the banking system of Europe. A widespread crisis of confidence in the European banks caused by a series of sovereign defaults could make the U.S. financial crisis in 2008 look like child's play.

And it may be just around the corner.

Who Bears the Losses?

We know that a string of devaluations by some of Europe's weaker countries would cause a major capital deficiency among the largest European banks, which collectively hold 1.9 *trillion* euros of European sovereign debt. A crisis of confidence in major European banks simply cannot be allowed to happen, lest it bring down the world's financial system in a death spiral. Clearly, as part of a process to unhook some member countries from the euro currency zone while restructuring the eurozone, a parallel effort must be made to ensure the viability of the affected banks.

The likely course of action will be a separate meeting between the leadership of the European Union and the heads of all major European banks. The damage will be assessed using assumptions as to which countries will devalue upon exiting the eurozone. Then the effect on each bank will be discussed and assessed. In the end, the European community as a whole will be under considerable pressure to guarantee the obligations of the European banks to ensure their survival and avoid a panic. But what does that mean? It means that, in effect, the European Union will be asked to subsidize the defaults of the departing members since most of the debt that will be restructured is owned by the banks.

But not so fast. The total cost of this bailout will resemble the American bailout of the banks in 2008 and 2009. At this point, there will be considerable pressure by the governments to resist a full bailout. Discussions will conclude that the cost of the bailouts should be shared between the issuing nations, the rescuing nations, and the bondholders. A powerful argument will be made that bondholders should also share in the eventual losses.

The result will be that European governments will collectively determine how the pain gets shared. How much will bondholders lose? How much financial damage will the bailed out countries endure? No matter the eventual formulas, the strong eurozone countries, mostly France and Germany, will own the banks they don't already own as a condition for the necessary bailout. The others will be indebted to the European Union for many years. This may not be a good time to own shares of European banks.

Expect that in an era of instant communications and few secrets, markets will react violently and negatively to rumors that the eurozone is coming apart fueled by a series of impending devaluations. Markets abhor uncertainty, and in terms of uncertainty and fear, this crisis is a 10 out of 10. Worldwide equity markets will sink on heavy volume and bond markets will virtually shut down. Indeed, where are the buyers of Greek or Irish debt going to come from? The euro will plunge and come close to parity with the U.S. dollar in a frenetic week or so of trading.

The Euro Implodes—or Does It?

Let's imagine that at the meeting outside Brussels, the leaders come to statesmanlike decisions as they recognize the realities they all face. The weak members will never be able to abide by the rules of the European Union. Alas, the world has changed, debt has increased, and there is no austerity path out that makes any sense, so five or six of the eurozone nations agree to drop out. Without saying it out loud, they all know that the reforms of their economy will require a fresh start that will begin with a devaluation of their new currency, which will most likely be their old currency. Greece will revive its drachma, Spain its peseta, Ireland its pound/punt, and so forth. These changes are complicated, of course, and switching a national currency involves a massive amount of planning for large and small details. The new currency must be designed and printed; exchange of currency must be organized and implemented. The new exchange rate will reflect the devaluation needed by each departing country.

The Euro Emerges Stronger, and the Crisis Moves across the Atlantic

When the dust clears and announcements are made by the EU leadership, some degree of order will return. The eurozone might include a smaller number of nations, down from 16 to 10 or 11, but the remaining countries will be stronger than the departing countries. Not surprisingly, the euro will rise against the dollar and other currencies. Stock markets will begin to recover. Bond markets will trade anew. Greece, Ireland, Portugal, and Spain will devalue by virtue of establishing a fresh exchange rate for their new currency now that they are no longer part of the euro system. Bankers will breathe a sigh of relief, even those who find themselves now working for a European government, the bank's new owner, rather than their old shareholders. Some may even find this an attractive tradeoff.

When a form of calm returns to the European financial markets, savvy investors will turn their attention to the next financial powder keg. They won't have to look far. The most financially precarious nation on earth is also the world's most important.

Chapter 6

The Crisis Hits the United States

By now, four European countries have abandoned the euro and readopted their old currency at a rate of exchange that signals a major devaluation when compared to the old rate of exchange with the euro. While the crisis eases in Europe, the world's attention turns to the nation that has the biggest impending problem with its budget and national finances: the United States.

In Chapter 1, we discussed the financial crisis facing the United States. Normally, a growing crisis attracts increasing attention. But for some reason, that does not happen in the United States. Many informed voices rail about the impending fiscal crisis, but these voices are ignored. Our national debt keeps mounting, our deficits increase, and no one seems to care. Some voices are raised in Congress, but they are not loud enough or persuasive enough to prompt the type of legislative action that is needed. Indeed, solving the problem involves sacrifice, and for most members of Congress, sacrifice is not a sure road to reelection, especially if the sacrifice is to come from your constituents. So, as it has been so many times in the past, the problem is ignored until it is right on the doorstep. Well, dear friends and elected officials, someone is knocking.

We are not writing an economic treatise with this book. Our idea is to make the problems clear and understandable to the informed and concerned reader, and rather than deluge you with statistics, we will point out only the most dramatic facts we need for making the point. Let's start with a quote:

> *A growing level of federal debt would also increase the probability of a sudden fiscal crisis, during which investors would lose confidence in the government's ability to manage its budget, and the government would thereby lose its ability to borrow at affordable rates. It is possible that interest rates would rise gradually as investors' confidence declined . . . but as other countries' experiences show, it is also possible that investors would lose confidence abruptly and interest rates on government debt would rise sharply.*[1]

The prose is stilted, but the message is clear: The federal debt is at a level where a sudden fiscal crisis may be imminent and interest rates could rise dramatically. As if that weren't scary enough, consider the source: the Congressional Budget Office. The paper tells us that the federal debt held by the public was at 62 percent of GDP at the end of fiscal year 2010, having risen from 36 percent at the end of fiscal year 2007, just before the recession began. Then it points out: "In only one other period in U.S. history—during and shortly after World War II—has that figure exceeded 50%."

So we are in relatively uncharted waters. But what does it mean?

We might draw several conclusions without venturing into the area of wild guesses. The conclusions are obvious consequences of where we are and where we are going. Let's use the CBO's projections as a starting point. Recall that the CBO is a nonpartisan government economic think tank. It is part of Congress, but as a nonpartisan group, it is not supposed to put any kind of spin on its reports. As the old baseball umpire said, we call 'em as we see 'em. As we pointed out in Chapter 1, according to the CBO, "federal debt held by the public will stand at 62 percent of GDP at the end of fiscal year 2010, having risen from 36 percent at the end of fiscal year 2007, just before the recession began." At over 60 percent of GDP, that would be the highest level since 1952. Then the CBO, holding back no punches, says: "As a result, interest payments on the debt are poised to skyrocket; the government's spending on net interest will triple between 2010 and 2020, increasing from $207 billion to $723 billion." (In a later paper published in December 2010, the CBO raised the 2020 figure to $778 billion.[2])

If you think that's scary, hold on to your hat. It gets much, much worse. First, remember that these projections are based on the budget deficit. The deficit is composed of estimates for revenues minus expenditures. A deficit of $1.3 trillion just means that we spent $1.3 trillion more than we took in. So to believe any future estimate of deficits, we need to believe the revenue and expenditures estimates on which they are based. Pretty simple. But do you believe the CBO's estimates of government revenues?

We don't.

We believe that the government revenues will be *far lower* than anticipated. We touched on this earlier in the book, but it is worth repeating.

The growth rates of GDP that the CBO projects in 2012, 2013, and 2014 are all in excess of 5 percent, ranging from 5.3 percent to 5.9 percent. We think this is not only unrealistic, but it also is wildly optimistic! Remember that consumer spending accounts for nearly 70 percent of GDP. With unemployment hovering around 9 percent, we think it is highly unlikely that GDP is going to grow at rates of 5 percent-plus! That means that the CBO's revenue projections are also wildly optimistic, since without strong growth there will be lower tax receipts than estimated, and therefore there will be a much larger deficit than estimated. Just to give you an idea of the scale of the deficits and what they might represent, we are talking about annual deficits well over $1 trillion as far as the eye can see. In February 2011, President Obama announced that the estimate of the current year's deficit had risen to $1.6 trillion, the highest in history. That's more than the entire annual discretionary budget of the U.S. government. The entire Medicare annual budget is $450 billion. The *combined* budgets of the Departments of Education, Energy, Justice, Homeland Security, Transportation, Veteran Affairs, and even State total less than $600 billion! As anyone can see, fixing the budget is a daunting task. We'll have some ideas on how to do it in a later chapter.

Here's another problem with the CBO's estimates. We just saw that the CBO projects that by 2020 the cost of servicing the debt could jump to $778 billion. As staggering a figure as that is, it assumes only a moderate rise in interest rates. Sorry to say, but we believe that interest rates are going to rise—perhaps dramatically—as will inflation, so the $778 billion cost to service the debt is also likely very understated. If you are starting to get a queasy feeling, we share your pain.

Doing the Math

Like in any good horror movie, we saved the truly scariest for last. It is the interest on the debt. We just mentioned that the CBO estimates that the cost of servicing the national debt could rise to $778 billion by 2020. Then we pointed out that the number may actually be understated, given that it assumes relatively mild inflation and relatively stable interest rates. What if those benign assumptions are wrong? The CBO helped us out with that, too:

> *For example, a 4-percentage-point across-the-board increase in interest rates would raise federal payments next year by about $100 billion relative to CBO baseline projection—a jump of more than 40 percent. . . . by 2015, if such higher-than-anticipated rates persisted, net interest would be nearly double the roughly $460 billion that the CBO currently projects for that year.*[3]

Think about it. Our very own Congressional Budget Office is telling us that if interest rates were to go up, say, 4 percent—a prospect we consider quite likely and possibly even conservative—by 2015, which is just around the corner, the annual interest payments alone on our national debt would be about *one trillion dollars!* One trillion dollars is roughly the same amount the federal government currently collects annually in individual income taxes. Can we imagine a situation where 100 percent of what we pay in individual income taxes goes to servicing our national debt?

We'll wait while you catch your breath.

The Congressional Budget Office walks a fine line between telling it like it is and raising the ire of everyone in Congress and the administration. How does it accomplish this? In this case, it has not one, but *two* sets of projections. The first is called the Extended Baseline Scenario, what we might call the "Gee-we-wish-this-would-really-happen scenario." Under this scenario, annual budget deficits would decline over the coming years and deficits and debt would remain stable for a number of years. Debt would equal 80 percent of GDP by 2035; that's not a great result, but it's likely not catastrophic either.

The second scenario is called the Alternative Fiscal Scenario, the one we might call the "Scared-to-death-this-might-really-happen scenario," which might also have a "We-told-you-so" postscript. Under this scenario, the outlook gets really rough. The CBO's assumptions are that the 2001 and 2003 tax cuts are extended indefinitely (in late December 2010, Congress passed a bill extending the tax cuts for everyone for two additional years), the alternative minimum tax is indexed for inflation, Medicare's payments to physicians rise (which does not happen under current law), and tax revenues remain at about 19 percent of GDP.

Figure 6.1 shows federal debt held by the public from 1790 to 2035, and it shows both scenarios beginning in 2010. Let's focus on the Alternative Fiscal Scenario.

Under the more pessimistic scenario, by 2020 *external* debt (not including the internal debt such as the funds the government borrows from Social Security, which also have to be repaid) would equal nearly 90 percent of GDP. Economists Ken Rogoff and Carmen Reinhart

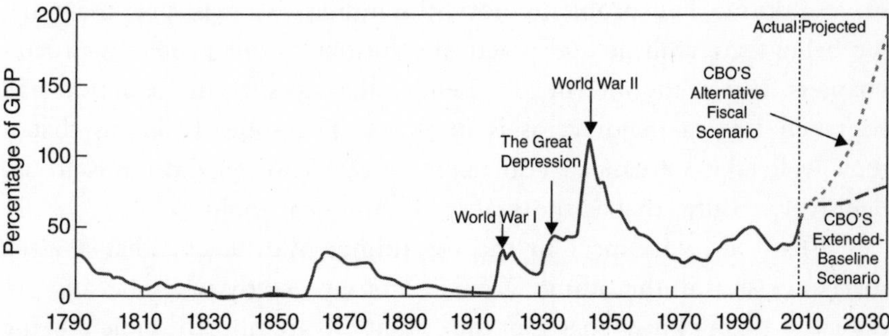

Figure 6.1 Federal Debt Held by the Public, 1790–2035 (percentage of GDP)

Source: Congressional Budget Office, "The Long-Term Budget Outlook" (June 2010); "Historical Data on Federal Debt Held by the Public" (July 2010).

pointed out that advanced economies have experienced slower growth through history when their debt-to-GDP ratio exceeds 90 percent. (Here we are talking about total debt, internal and external, not just the debt held by individuals and foreign governments.[4]) At debt levels above 90 percent, a developed country's growth typically slowed to 1.6 percent. Well, we are just about at the 90 percent level (internal and external debt) and expected to be above 100 percent in 2012. The sad reality is that if the United States grows at no more than 2 percent, we have virtually no chance of reducing our unemployment below 9 percent. (Generally, a 3 percent increase in output corresponds to a 1 percent decline in the rate of unemployment.[5])

Under the Alternative scenario, debt held by the public (again, not counting the internal government borrowings) would reach a record high of about 110 percent of GDP in 2025 and would rise to an intolerable 180 percent of GDP in 2035. We dare not even attempt to calculate the interest cost, and the percentage of GDP it would consume, should these debt levels be attained.

What Have We Learned?

It is clear that the United States is on the path to a fiscal train wreck. The sources we have cited are not obscure gloom-and-doom prognosticators, but serious economists and, most of all, the Congressional Budget Office. The problems we face are so severe that there is no easy solution. The problems notwithstanding, we will propose what we believe are realistic and practical solutions to our problems in later chapters. But in the interim, we believe that no substantive action will be taken until a major crisis is upon us. The sober reality is that it may well take a financial equivalent of 9/11 to get Congress to act decisively. Sadly, that is the reality of American politics.

What can we expect in the meantime? We believe that a stock market crash is in the offing. We dare not say exactly when because, of course, we can't know that. But the conditions are ripe; the table is being set for a calamitous financial event that will eclipse the 2008 debacle.

Here is how it is likely to unfold. Once the troubles in Europe have exploded and the world's attention is rife with serial devaluations, attention will focus on similar and even worse problems faced by the

United States. Our out-of-control trillion-dollar-plus deficits will finally attract world scrutiny. In the United States, the printing presses will continue to roll at smoking-hot speed while the Fed attempts to keep interest rates low in the face of the Treasury's continued borrowing and the importance of enabling low-cost mortgages for the moribund housing market.

As the world takes in what is happening, interest rates will rise. The financial markets will no longer be prepared to accept the risk of lending in U.S. dollars at paltry interest rates. The trillions of dollars of quantitative easing will regurgitate in the form of more money chasing fewer goods. The Treasury will continue to borrow because it has to, but at higher and higher rates. The CBO's Alternative plan is coming true with a vengeance. (Recall that quantitative easing involves the Fed's purchase of government bonds with new money it creates. The effect is to increase the money supply and lower interest rates in the short term.)

In this environment, investors will be wary of paper assets and trend toward higher allocations to real assets. Gold will continue to climb. (In the next section, we will discuss specific investment strategies for the troubled times ahead.)

To go back to Nassim Nicholas Taleb and his admonition against predictions that can be characterized as "epistemic arrogance," we cannot in all honesty predict the timing and specific trigger for a stock market event. But we might venture an opinion anyway. While stock market volatility will inevitably spike during a period of great financial uncertainty, the trigger for a crash—our guess, at least—is likely to be a failed Treasury auction. Let us explain.

The U.S. Treasury sells government securities (bond, bills, and notes) to the public through open auctions. There are two types of bidders: competitive and noncompetitive. The competitive bidders are mostly primary dealers who have a direct relationship with the Federal Reserve. Noncompetitive bidders are generally individual investors. They always get their securities, but they have to accept the yield that is determined by the bids of the competitive bidders. The competitive bidders submit bids based on the yield they are willing to accept. The winners are those that offered the lowest yield first, and then the Treasury goes through the list, accepting higher bids until they sell all the securities they want to sell. All of the winning bidders get the highest yield that was accepted. (This is a very simplified version of how these auctions occur.) The Treasury has never failed to find buyers for its securities since there are no better credits than the United States of America. In fact, when the auction is complete, a summary identifies the interest rate and the "bid-to-cover," which is the amount of oversubscription for the issue. In other words, a bid-to-cover of 3 means that there were three times as many bidders for the securities as were offered. Indeed, a bid-to-cover of 3 times is considered good and is fairly common.

But as the crisis deepens, the Treasury still needs to borrow. Wall Street observes that in the subsequent auctions, the bid-to-cover ratios decline steadily, from 3 to 2.5, to 2 and then to under 2. Now the alarm bells start to ring. The financial community watches nervously as the Treasury prepares a large auction of 10-year bonds. Investors know that if the bonds don't sell well, there will be a massive wave of fear.

And while Wall Street holds its breath, the auction fails.

There are simply not enough buyers who have the confidence to buy the U.S. securities given the poisonous atmosphere. The first reaction is that interest rates spike and go to 8 percent, 10 percent, and higher. Investors, spooked by the Treasury's historic difficulty in selling bonds, sense an impending collapse in the economy and start to pull their money out of risk assets. With Treasuries unstable and inflation about to soar, they get out of stocks and bonds and run for cover. Gold and a few other commodities soar on the influx of scared money.

Banks brace for the worst. A run on the banks is feared. The Federal Reserve and the FDIC try to reassure investors that their money is safe, but emotions run high and lines form outside the branches of major banks.

As everyone feared, the stock market crashes. The market suffers its worst fall since the crash on October 19, 1987, when the market declined more than 22 percent in a single day.

The crisis is upon us; it is the worst financial crisis in U.S. history.

Chapter 7

The Way Back

Now that we've come this far down the wrong path, it's time to find the way back to prosperity. While we've diagnosed the myriad problems of sovereign debt, onerous deficits, and profligate spending that will bring down the U.S. economy, we also believe there are solutions. To be sure, there are no easy answers, but a dedication to fiscal common sense and monetary discipline is the right place to start as we seek to end this death spiral.

Over the past 20 years we've seen an economy essentially driven by asset bubbles—the dot-com craze in the 1990s, followed by the speculation-fueled real estate frenzy in the 2000s. The mother's milk of all bubbles is extremely accommodative monetary policy, which we've had in abundance. The dollar spigots have been turned to full pressure, and the results have been predictable—wild surges in asset prices followed by crippling crashes, each one taking more and more out of the economy. Grievous policy errors at all levels have brought us to where we are, so now it's time to start looking for answers.

Strengthening the States

The governors who have helped steward the United States through a decade of profligate spending and mercilessly regressive tax policies might not seem a logical place to start when one would go looking for solutions. But that was precisely what the *Wall Street Journal* did on October 13, 2010, polling four high-profile governors from debt-plagued states to explain how they were rallying their jurisdictions back from the brink.[1] The essay was introduced entirely without irony and with little commentary or introduction, save for a staid label headline proclaiming, "Four Governors on How to Cut Spending." The governors were Ed Rendell, the Democrat from Pennsylvania and former head of the national party; Arnold Schwarzenegger, the high-profile Republican "Governator" of California; Deval Patrick, the free-spending Democrat from Massachusetts; and Bob McDonnell, Virginia's newcomer Republican, who at the time of the *Journal* essay was already having his name bandied around as a national ticket candidate for the Grand Old Party.

McDonnell quickly established fiscally hawkish credentials during his first year in office by erasing $1.8 billion annual and $4.2 billion biennial budget deficits, using an aggressive array of spending cuts and eschewing tax increases that many on the left thought unavoidable to rescue the Old Dominion State. As for his other three writing partners—well, let's just say their decided lack of bona fides raised questions about why we would be taking fiscal advice from any of these guys.

Besides writing on the same *Journal* Op-Ed page, the three have something else in common: They each received grades of D on the Cato Institute's Fiscal Policy Report Card on America's Governors for 2010. Cato is a libertarian think tank whose analysts, while occasionally taking somewhat naïve positions on how much government can be realistically eradicated from our lives, look closely at how well public officials deliver the goods when it comes to keeping the size of government in check. Three of our four essayists don't measure up well, and with good reason.

"The lowest scoring governors are those who have increased taxes and spending the most," the report states. "With the poor economy of recent years, these governors have pursued large tax increases in their efforts to balance state budgets. Unfortunately, these policies damage the economy and hurt families and businesses at a time when they can least afford it."[2]

Despite a lingering air of hypocrisy, the opinion piece is instructive in that it exemplifies how relatively simple it is to diagnose the illness and how politically complicated and obscure the solution can be. Ed Rendell—Pennsylvania's "Fast Eddie," whose part-time job is giving postgame analysis on a local cable channel for pro football's Philadelphia Eagles—is as good a poster child as any for just how difficult it can be to transfer political rhetoric into practical solutions.

Rendell's commentary starts with the proclamation that "Pennsylvania now spends $2 billion less to run state government than it did eight years ago." The statement is a cynical fairy tale that might lead the reader to conclude that the loquacious governor had actually cut spending during his two terms in office. Nothing could be further from the truth. While Rendell may have managed to trim the actual size of running the government itself, spending and taxation increased dramatically during his tenure, far offsetting $14 million in savings he touted on office supplies and attempts to rein in the state's runaway pension fund. Republican Governor Mark Schweiker presented Rendell with a $20.9 billion balanced general fund budget when he left office at the beginning of 2003, which Rendell ballooned into a $28.05 billion pork-laden mess, complete with $41.8 billion of total debt.

Lest we be called overly cynical, we do tip our hat to Rendell for some common-sense savings measures. Like other conglomerates both public and private, Pennsylvania has gone to work to figure out how to rein in health-care costs, an especially vital consideration now that ObamaCare looms as a trip hammer for governments and businesses trying to protect their bottom lines. Whatever you think of the president's Patient Protection and Affordable Care Act, it is undeniable that while it may provide care to millions, the cost for state governments will be enormous. Millions will flock to state-funded Medicaid programs and add to the staggering costs of the nation's $2.3 trillion health-care industry. So while wellness plans, such as the Pennsylvania incentive that encourages healthier living, are unlikely to bring actual reductions to anyone's health-care costs, they are a viable approach toward at least keeping increases down—to an annual hike of 7 percent in Pennsylvania's case.

For Governor Schwarzenegger, as is the case with many other elected leaders looking to control costs, the prime focus was pensions. While politicians bemoan the bonuses given to Wall Street executives, many for too long have failed to touch the delicate issue of public pensions for fear of alienating unions and their powerful lobbyists. If Social Security is the third rail of American politics, then union pensions are the overhead wires on the train tracks. But the time has come when the issue no longer can be ignored.

In California's case, the state spent $6.5 billion on retirement costs in 2010, marking the first time that figure eclipsed the considerable cost of higher education. Through some deft politicking, Schwarzenegger won some concessions: increased employee contributions to pension funds; a rollback in pension levels for new hires to pre-1999 levels; an end to pension "spiking" in which employees finagle higher pensions at the end of their careers; and opening up the pension accounting system for greater public scrutiny. Schwarzenegger excoriates politicians on both sides of the aisle who think higher taxes are the only solution, and he offers a salient observation: "[P]rivate sector job growth will be enhanced if public-sector retirement benefits are brought under control. All it takes is some lawmakers who are willing to stand up to the special interests and do what's right."

In Governor Deval Patrick's case, his checkered history when it comes to frugality is slowly, and we emphasize slowly, being mitigated as his state adopts pro-growth policies that make sense. While he endorsed an economically regressive increase in the state sales tax to 6.25 percent from 5 percent, it is heartening to see the state cut the business tax rate to 8.75 percent from 9.5 percent. Patrick speaks freely of "investing" in various parts of the economy—an endeavor that can be a code word for "taxing"—but the government also has seen some common-sense consolidations and privatizing of public jobs, one small example being the use of civilian flaggers instead of expensive police details for construction projects. These are minute measures, but perhaps a journey of many fiscal miles does begin with the first step.

Virginia, though, has been taking big steps. Governor Bob McDonnell did what Deval Patrick could not—close a budget deficit without the benefit of a tax increase. In fact, McDonnell faced down the state Legislature, which had been set to approve a $2 billion tax increase proposed by the previous administration. McDonnell's tenure has been checkered somewhat by his refusal to disavow the state's Confederate past, but there is little disputing the fiscal progress Virginia has made.

Like his counterpart in California, McDonnell has attacked the pension system, mandating employee contributions "for the first time in a generation," a move estimated to save $3 billion over 10 years. The state also has instituted a hiring freeze of public workers, another savings of $20 million a year. He also has established a commission to evaluate more than one thousand cost-saving ideas, primarily focusing on streamlining government operations. (No, we are not ignorant of the irony involved with spending money on a panel to find ways to save money, but this is what you would classify as a necessary evil.) Finally, McDonnell is addressing state spending needs, primarily on road projects, by proposing the long-overdue privatization of the state liquor system and conducting an audit of the transportation department. "We intend to redo the way government operates," McDonnell wrote.

Government sure does need a redo, and there's no better place to start than with the fiscal policies that have brought us to this desperate point. Reversing those policies and charting a brighter course toward sustainable prosperity with controlled inflation is still possible, and that topic will take the focus of the rest of this chapter as we highlight additional ways beyond the above-mentioned fixes to heal our economy. Austerity and good fiscal sense are the cornerstone of our remedies, but those approaches require more than rhetoric; they require action. Let's start with the nexus of all the problems in the United States: the destruction of the dollar.

Bring Back the Buck

This book has gone to great lengths to explain the sad recent history of the U.S. currency and the Federal Reserve's reckless resolve to destroy the dollar. Despite Ben Bernanke's rightful recognition as one of the nation's leading scholars on the Great Depression, the Fed chairman has proceeded headlong on a path to rewrite three millennia of economic history that clearly shows you cannot devalue your way to prosperity, no matter how enticing short-term gains may appear.

In pursuing its zero interest rate policy, also known as ZIRP, the Fed sought to stimulate the economy through an unofficial policy of devaluing the dollar. A weaker greenback makes goods cheaper in relative terms and stimulates exports, something the United States badly needed after the housing market collapsed and took the financial system with it. Make no mistake, the cheap dollar had some desired effect. Exports increased sharply from the fourth quarter of 2009 through the third quarter of 2010. Industrial supply exports rose 20.2 percent, capital goods by 17 percent, autos by 63.2 percent, consumer goods by 9.6 percent, and miscellaneous other goods by 16.7 percent, according to Deutsche Bank's Global Markets Research. These numbers should not be dismissed blithely, and the Fed does deserve a degree of credit for jumpstarting the economy and bringing the stock market off its vastly oversold lows of March 2009.

However, the central bank's great mistake was never planning a viable exit strategy. As Chairman Bernanke and his cohort are well aware, stimulative measures need most of all to be two things: targeted and temporary. Otherwise, they create an unsustainable dependence on artificial backstops and cheap money, as all of that cash in the system will create inflation unless it is properly controlled. The Fed has tried to create organic demand where there is none, instead of letting the economy adjust to the pace of real demand and behave accordingly. An ancillary effect is the risk of a trade war, to which global competitive currency devaluation always will ultimately lead. All of these factors combined have but one result: a crash.

The Fed can halt this madness by giving the markets a little shock therapy. It needs to be as bold with raising rates as it was with cutting them. At some point the economy is going to have to take the training wheels off, and it is the Fed's obligation to step aside or risk sending the message that the United States is incapable of recovering on its own. If the downturn has in part been a crisis of confidence—and we strongly believe it is—then Chairman Bernanke must show that the central bank is ready to use some tough love and complete its handoff to the private sector. The Fed has a dual legal mandate—maintaining strong employment levels while keeping inflation under control. The current of economic fear and suppression of animal spirits has prevented the former objective from being realized, while the use of artificially low interest rates and the debasing of the currency will defeat the latter goal. Once Dr. Frankenstein's inflation monster gets off the laboratory table, Bernanke will be unable to control him.

Let's be clear: Volcker-level increases may be needed at some point, but probably not yet. The argument that the Great Depression was exacerbated in 1937 by too much tightening has some validity, and the Fed will have to take measured steps out of the monetary mire. But we hearken back to a woman named Susan Powter, a spike-haired ball of energy who in the 1990s boom days was one of the nation's premier diet gurus.

Her slogan then is ours now: "Stop the insanity!"

Stop the Presses

The next thing the Fed needs to do is halt its quantitative easing, or QE, measures. The term refers, at its core, to the Fed's "printing" money which it then uses to buy assets, most frequently Treasuries but also mortgage, credit card, and other debt. The Fed purchases the assets from institutions, which are then expected to leverage the money up and buy risk assets or lend out the funds. That in turn drives short-term growth through gains in the stock market and, ideally, by driving consumer and business loan demand. However, that extra cash comes with a price, and there is scant evidence to show that quantitative easing has done much to achieve its goal, which is to goose the economy by improving liquidity.

The case, in fact, is much clearer that QE has become a psychological tool that the Fed uses to tell the market that it's doing, well, something. As of this writing, the central bank has unleashed $2.4 trillion worth of easing into the economy. Yet indicators show that while the supply of money has been cruising along at a nice clip, the actual velocity of money has trailed. This is largely because corporations, particularly banks, have been squirreling away their money as the U.S. corporate balance sheet swelled to nearly $2 trillion.

And why should banks lend? With the Fed funds rate near zero and the benchmark 10-year Treasury note holding yields in the 3.25 percent range, why would a bank want to jeopardize such a healthy risk-free margin just to satisfy a bunch of bureaucrats who decided the best way out of a financial crisis is to find more ways to cheapen the money? Now, one might suggest that banks get more aggressive in the interest of magnanimity and egalitarianism and help get the economy rolling again, but banks aren't in business to be good corporate citizens. They're in it to make money, and if they can find a cheap way to do it without risking their necks—particularly after the worst three-year stretch in the industry's history—they're obviously going to take the easy way out.

Quantitative easing is supposed to encourage banks to lend to high-quality customers, who will invest that money in their businesses or just go to the mall and spend it on their kids. But a lack of confidence in the economy, caused by unemployment and the insane levels of debt and deficits strangling growth, has made lenders unwilling to lend and spenders unwilling to spend. The Fed is an integral part of this culture of fear, both through its ineffective policies and the naïve belief that there will not be a huge price to pay for the sequence of inflation-inducing QE measures. The central bank's ambivalence toward the dollar has taken root in a variety of measures, with consumers first to feel the pinch before the other more academic measures of inflation take hold.

One of the main features of our global inflation scenario is a sharp rise in commodity prices. Cheap greenbacks make dollar-denominated assets less expensive when compared to the foreign currencies used to buy them. We saw what happened during the first phase of the stock market crash, in 2008, as investors flocked from equities and used cheaper dollars to buy oil, sending crude to $147 a barrel and prices at the pump well past $4 a gallon.[3] The resulting price inflation added a huge tax onto ordinary consumers at a time when they could afford it least—as their 401(k) plans were turning into 201(k) plans and serious concerns arose over whether the heart of the U.S. economic system was irretrievably broken.

A rule of thumb is that for every one percentage point in decline for the dollar, oil rises $6 a barrel, which in turn causes a 3-cent-per-gallon rise at the pump. That 3-cent increase causes U.S. households to spend an extra $3 billion in energy consumption. That's also called a tax. This is but one nightmare awaiting consumers.

"The solution to inflation is the elimination of its cause," St. Louis Federal Reserve President Darryl R. Francis said in a 1971 speech. Francis rightly observed that the primary cause of inflation is directly tied to the rate of monetary growth. Francis delivered a valuable warning about the consequences of slow action, the type of which we have seen from modern-day policy makers. "The lag between appropriate monetary actions and the achievement of relatively stable prices may thus be expected to extend over a period of three to four years, following a prolonged and relatively high rate of monetary expansion," he said, later reemphasizing, "Excessive money growth is the cause of inflation, and a slower rate of money growth is the solution to the problem."

The economy will have enough inflation fear from the treacherous defaults ahead on sovereign debt, as well as the exported inflation from emerging market growth. It doesn't need the central bank piling on with money-printing. The Fed needs to abandon quantitative easing and stabilize the money supply.

Be Good Consumers and Good Savers

One of the most frustrating aspects of the recession has been the dichotomy between how the public and private sectors have reacted to the crisis. While the private sector has stopped spending and started saving, the public sector has taken the position that the best way out of our national malaise is through the hair of the dog that bit us. Think about it: When your household starts to feel a pinch and you realize that your economic condition is becoming perilous, what do you do? Do you start looking for ways to borrow more money so you can buy a new car and a flat-screen TV? Or do you take a hard look at your bills, compare it to your income, and come up with a plan to get you and your family back to financial health?

Now think about the government's response. When the financial system began to crumble, the first reaction was to find ways to get money flowing in the system—not an unreasonable response in that the economy surely was in need of growth, and the one way to spur that is through spending. But we would expect the government to treat its purchases with the same prudence that households treat theirs. More than $2 trillion of money-printing and a trillion-dollar-plus deficit later, it would be hard for anybody in Washington, Democrat or Republican, to make that case.

Hopefully, the issue of getting people with a stronger sense of fiscal and monetary sensibility in Washington will be settled at the ballot box. The November 2010 election made a strong statement on how passionately Americans feel about reforming the way business is done in the halls of political power. But that is only half the issue. The rest lies within the hearts of the public.

Yes, to a large extent the causes of our current predicament extend beyond the control of John and Jane Doe taxpayers. But Mr. and Mrs. Doe have gotten off easy in their roles as principal players in this drama. This is largely because one does not blame the victim. We don't fault the homeowner whose house has burned down nor the fellow whose car gets broadsided in the middle of an intersection. But what if the homeowners went out for the evening with candles burning near the dining room curtains? And what if that fellow who got broadsided had just rolled through a stop sign? We still empathize with their plight, but it makes sense to examine our own actions as they relate to sometimes-dire consequences.

For how much we show our indignation at Wall Street and all of the toxic recipes it cooked up to package and repackage mortgage securities, we also must recognize that none of this would have been possible without a compliant consumer. After all, someone was out there buying houses with NINJA—no income, no job or assets—loans just as surely as someone was selling them. Someone was out there treating their homes like piggy banks, leveraging and releveraging their mortgages to go out and buy those new cars and flat-screen TVs. All of this occurred as U.S. net savings rates hovered around zero or below, setting the table for disaster after the unthinkable—the cessation of property value increases—occurred and blew up those aforementioned securities that Wall Street used to bankroll the Awesome Aughts.

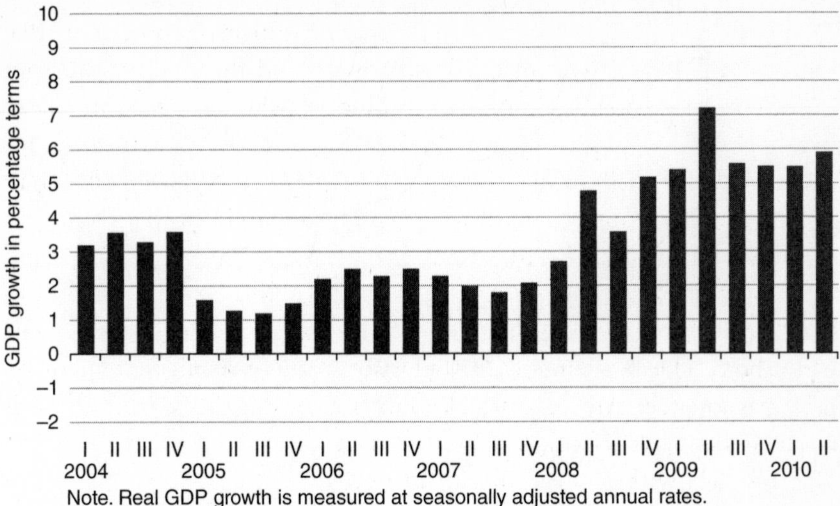

Figure 7.1 Personal Saving Rate as a Percentage of Disposable Personal Income
SOURCE: U.S. Bureau of Economic Analysis.

The desired epilogue is, of course, not for Americans to stop buying new cars and flat-screen TVs, both of which are wonderful to have, amplify the quality of life for their owners, and help drive the employment and business growth vital to our survival. But responsibility becomes the watchword, and for much of the previous decade Americans, quite frankly, ran up debt and depleted savings in a haphazard manner, to say the least.

Figure 7.1 provides a stark example of American saving trends. Note how low the rate dipped during the excesses of the real estate boom and rose when the worst of the credit crisis hit.

If we go back even further, we can see how poor we've become at saving, compared to the recovery days of the 1980s and to the excesses of the 1990s and the 2000s. As we can see in Figure 7.2, personal savings as a percentage of disposable income tumbled from 11 percent in 1982 to an anemic 1.4 percent in 2005 before rebounding to an 11-year high of 4.3 percent in 2009. An important point arises from this trend: We need not be out mortgaging the ranch and breaking the bank to generate healthy economic growth. To the contrary, saving spiked in the early 1980s as Paul Volcker took his

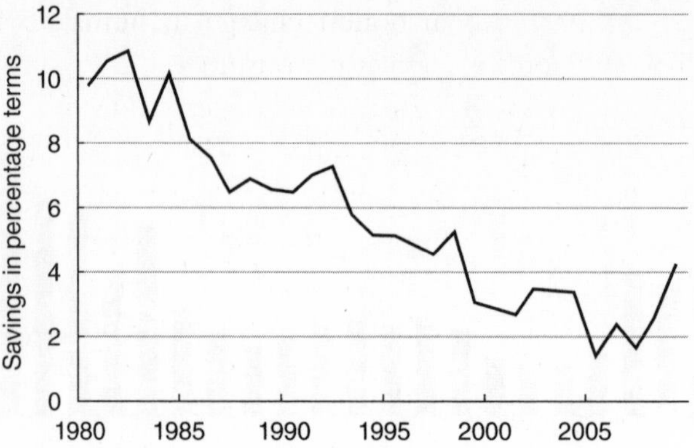

Figure 7.2 Personal Savings Rate as an Annualized Percentage
SOURCE: U.S. Bureau of Economic Analysis.

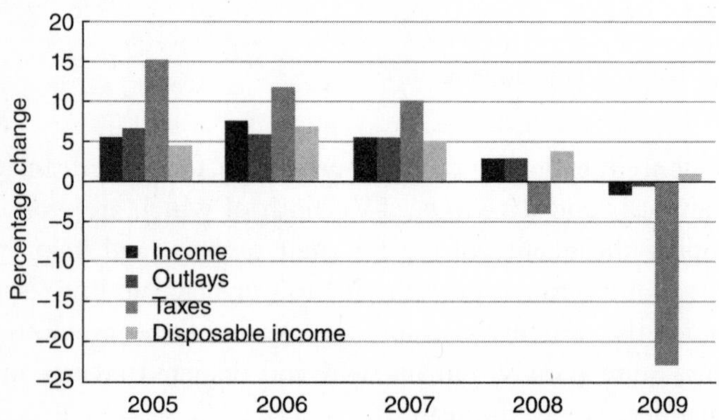

Figure 7.3 Percentage Change in Components of Personal Savings Rate
SOURCE: U.S. Bureau of Economic Analysis.

controversial steps to control inflation, but it kept up at a healthy rate during the Great Moderation of the 1990s before the dot-com bubble exploded and made way for the real estate bubble.

There are two primary reasons the personal savings rate has begun to rebound: an actual decrease in outlays and a gain on personal income due to the tax breaks of the 2008 and 2009 stimulus packages. Figure 7.3 depicts how the relationship has changed between the varying factors. The decrease in outlays is an organic phenomenon, which is to say it reflects an honest change in human behavior that denotes a real shift on behalf of the consumer.

The increase in savings that comes from a decrease in taxes is a less certain animal. With Washington of a mood to reduce or eliminate tax cuts, particularly among the higher-income and higher-producing members of society, whether the savings rate continues to rise is a shaky proposition. As noted by Daniel Carroll and Beth Mowry, economists at the Federal Reserve Bank of Cleveland:

> *One may wonder if this change in household savings signifies a long-lasting change in households' saving behavior. For now, the answer is not certain. Surely, some of the decline in consumption expenditures has been caused by the sizeable downward adjustments to households' net worth from the financial crisis. As the economy recovers and net worth increases, households may revert back to their previous low levels of saving. We cannot look to persistent increases in disposable income from tax breaks to keep increasing the personal savings rate either. The federal government cannot continue to shrink tax liabilities at the current rates because it must manage future budget challenges. Over the long term, increases in the personal savings rate must come from reductions in household consumption relative to income, not from short-run tax breaks.*[4]

The government has a second problem with the savings level. With interest rates near zero for plain-vanilla investments such as money markets and certificates of deposit, there is virtually no reason for Americans to save. While the presence of Keynesian animal spirits in the marketplace is desirable and important, so is the need for Americans to act responsibly with their money. John Maynard Keynes used the term *animal spirits* in his 1936 book, *The General Theory of Employment, Interest and Money,* to describe a kind of "naïve optimism" that would drive investors to take risks. Keynes spoke a bit less glowingly of such emotion-driven actions than some of his modern-day disciples when using the term, but he nonetheless considered such behavior critical in moving markets higher.

Zero-interest savings accounts make an unattractive option as the world gravitates faster and faster toward inflation. While the money retains its nominal value, it loses compared to inflation, making the Fed's ZIRP stance an even greater attack on real wealth of real people. These are problems that especially plague lower-wage earners and those on fixed income who are merely trying to enjoy their retirements and see their life savings earn an appreciable rate of interest. The absurdly low rates of the past three years have done profound damage to the wealth of responsible rainy-day savers who did nothing to create the current economic crisis but are suffering at its hands.

Setting the Right Example

Our journey through the causes and effects of hyperinflation and the extreme danger it poses to the American economy has taken us through time and around the world, from the days of the Roman emperor Diocletian through the rampant eurozone debt accrual leading to the massive defaults that will set the stage for runaway U.S. inflation. We have spent this chapter diagramming some common-sense solutions both on a proactive and reactive level. That brings us all the way back home, where we finally issue a call on government leaders throughout the world to end the evil cycle of debts and deficits that have brought us to this critical juncture.

Many noted economists have shuddered at similar suggestions of frugality, and they use history as their guide. Conventional wisdom is that the nation entered a second phase of the Great Depression in 1937 because Washington went overboard in trying to reduce the deficit, and all that frugality helped choke off the recovery. As we sadly remember, it was only the onset of World War II and the genesis of the military-industrial complex that helped rejuvenate growth.

While we're perfectly cognizant of the common threads between this economy and the Depression-era slowdown—excessive speculation, wildly unregulated markets, and an overconfidence in risk assets—we also note their differences. The massive debt deleveraging and the far more global makeup of the current economy are but two of the most significant contrasts between now and then, and their presence necessitates a different worldview. To illustrate, we make a third note about the personal savings rate.

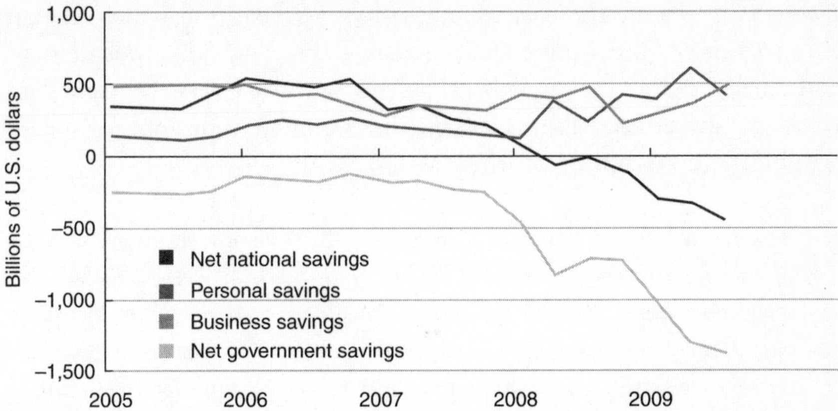

Figure 7.4 Net National Savings and Its Components (Quarterly, 2005:Q1 to 2009:Q3)
SOURCE: U.S. Bureau of Economic Analysis.

As we previously stated, personal savings has rebounded somewhat over the past year or two as tax cuts in the stimulus bills have returned some money to taxpayers. In real-money terms, however, that frugality has been almost completely offset by a negative savings rate in the government, due to reliance on foreign sources to fund U.S. fiscal policies. Figure 7.4 examines the relationship.

As you can see, the net government savings level has been a drag on the real amount of money we as Americans keep in reserves. Personal savings represents 55 percent of net savings for the past 30 years, but because national savings consist of personal, business and government activity, the government's use of foreign financing of its deficits has completely offset the private sector's efforts. In 2008, for the first time since the Great Depression, national savings turned negative, fueled not only by pressures on the consumer but also by the way in which the federal budget deficit is destroying the efforts of average people to right the country's economic ship.

Economist Nouriel Roubini, who has shared the Dr. Doom sobriquet with Marc Faber and was one of the few who accurately diagnosed the collapse of the financial system, writes of dire currency consequences in his cogent and timely book, *Crisis Economics: A Crash*

Course in the Future of Finance. He envisions a scenario in which foreign investors tire of the asinine U.S. deficits, debts, and dollar debasement and finally dump the greenback as the world's reserve currency in favor of something else, such as the Chinese renminbi or yuan. Roubini and co-author Stephen Mihm wrote:

> *The United States stands at a crossroads. If it doesn't get its fiscal house in order and increase its private savings, such a seismic event will only become more likely. It's all too easy to imagine a scenario where this plays out, particularly if a political stalemate develops: Republicans veto tax increases, Democrats veto spending cuts, and monetizing the deficits—printing money—becomes the path of least resistance. The resulting inflation will erode the dollar value of the public and private debt held around the world. Faced with such an "inflation tax," investors around the world dump their dollars, moving them into the currency of a country with a far better reputation for fiscal responsibility.*[5]

It can be of little wonder, then, that the national mood has turned so sour toward a government that has shown a complete lack of willingness to follow basic societal conventions when it comes to money management. It makes the situation all the more difficult when the government seems unable or unwilling to admit the extent to which its policies will lead to inflation sooner rather than later. The above scenario, in which Congress becomes politically emasculated and the Federal Reserve is left as the only policy body that can act, is another devastating episode likely to appear in our national nightmare.

Americans know inflation is coming, even though they might not know its exact origin or trigger. They see it at the supermarket and they see it at the gas pump and are tired of the government using ginned-down calculations in the Consumer Price Index trying to tell them that inflation is trending low. The constant denials about the threat inflation poses ring more and more hollow as the torrent of money about to flood the economy combines with the threat of mass sovereign debt defaults to drive rates higher and send the cost of living through the ceiling. Occasionally, though, someone in a policy-making position gets it right:

> *Deposit institutions are holding over a trillion dollars of excess reserves (that is, over 15 times what they are required to hold given their deposits). These excess reserves create the potential for high inflation. Suppose that households believe that prices will rise. They would then demand more deposits to use for transactions. Banks can readily accommodate this extra demand, because they are holding so many excess reserves. These extra deposits become extra money chasing the same amount of goods and so generate upward pressure on prices. The households' inflationary expectations would, in fact, become self-fulfilling.*[6]

These words were spoken on February 16, 2010, by Federal Reserve Bank of Minnesota President Narayana R. Kocherlakota and were an oasis of reason amid a desert of denial by Fed Chairman Bernanke and his minions when it comes to inflation. Kocherlakota went on to explain that 30 percent of all public debt is held in private hands, and for the government to pay off on all those Treasury bonds and notes it will have to either raise taxes or monetize the deficit through the printing of money. With little public appetite for higher taxes, the Fed will be forced to start the printing presses again, a move that will only stoke the fires of intractable inflation.

Where, then, do we stand? At the outset we made it clear that certain unalterable facts, particularly those concerning massive sovereign debt that ultimately will be restructured, combined with crushing debt and deficit burdens in the United States, make some sort of crash inevitable. The severity of the crash is yet to be determined, but there is no underestimating the importance of being prepared.

The American political and economic systems are at a precipice. Voters made their sentiments heard loud and clear in November 2010 when they rejected the ruling regime and turned the reins over to a new group whose members promised that the lessons of the past decade would not be forgotten. The chorus of pledges against profligate spending, reckless risk, and arbitrary bailouts resonated through the land, giving hope that our many mistakes will not be forgotten.

But we've heard this before, and we wonder whether we won't be subject to the same phenomenon observed so presciently in The Who's "Won't Get Fooled Again" rock anthem: "Meet the new boss/ same as the old boss." The new boss will face as daunting a set of challenges as the country has ever witnessed, without benefit of a road map or compass other than common sense and, hopefully, purposeful compassion for those who will weather the storms outlined here. In her brilliant book *The Forgotten Man*, Amity Shlaes describes the ones left behind during the Great Depression:

> *He was the Depression-era man who was not part of any political constituency and therefore lived the negatives of the period. He was the man who paid for the big projects, who got make-work instead of real work. He was the man who waited for economic growth that did not come.*[7]

Indeed, that person is likely to be found in droves as the economy weathers the massively inflationary period ahead. And he will need as much help from the wisdom of "the new boss" as he can get.

"American exceptionalism" has been a concept bandied about over the past few election cycles, and it will be needed more than ever in the time to come. The term refers to the abilities of Americans to rise above our many challenges and innovate our way back to prosperity, even when the odds seem impossibly daunting and as the system appears to many eyes to be broken. The United States has found itself at the crossroads of a crisis because of both its own largesse and its ignorance of history, as well as from the recklessness of foreign governments that borrowed and spent in an effort to provide excessive social services well beyond their capacity. Turning this ocean liner of woes around will be no easy or quick task, but we think Americans and their capacity for exceptionalism are up to the task.

Chapter 8

Forging Ahead

I admire your notion of fair odds, mister.
— Bernardo O'Reilly, *The Magnificent Seven*

This is hardly the first time a nation has faced seemingly intractable inflation brought on through the twin evils of debt and deficits, and it certainly won't be the last. A stroll through the history of inflation, from the Holy Roman Empire through the Weimar Republic and more recently to the "malaise days" of the 1970s has seen governments build their economies on quicksand and fight vainly to recover. In fact, the analogy is an effective one: When one is drifting ever lower in quicksand, sometimes the battling and struggling only makes matters worse. And so it goes for the world now. As debts and deficits pull world economies ever lower, the temptation to do, well, something can be an overwhelming and ultimately counterproductive endeavor.

The world and more specifically the United States has pursued a hair-of-the-dog-that-bit-you strategy in trying to solve its recession problems, and in doing so has merely laid the groundwork for a worse problem—inflation—down the road. As William F. Ford, former president of the Atlanta Federal Reserve, told the *New York Times* in October 2010 before a summit at Jekyll Island, Georgia, on the history of the central bank: "They're setting the stage for an outbreak of real serious inflation one or two years from now, at which point they will have no choice but to sell securities and raise interest rates, which will reduce the value of their assets and consequently their earnings."[1]

Ford's statement was a banker's way of saying that fundamental laws of supply and demand will dictate that when the Fed starts selling the nearly $3 trillion in assets it has accumulated, it will have to reward buyers with higher rates. That will set off an inflationary spiral as the Fed will have to take a loss on what it spent initially to buy all the Treasuries, mortgages, credit card debt, and assorted other purchases it made during its efforts to escape the quicksand of economic contraction. Couple that with the inflation from sovereign debt defaults and the soaring prices of goods that will come with dollar debasement and emerging market demand, and the stage will be set for crippling inflation. The temptation to do something, anything, will come back to bite and bite hard.

The great irony of this predicament is that Fed Chairman Ben Bernanke fancies himself quite the student of history. It is truly an experience to hear him recount the lessons of the Great Depression and why inaction from policy makers exacerbated the economic woes of the late 1920s and 30s. Yet it is also a source of great befuddlement that no one in Washington is willing to see that while extraordinary measures were required in some part to save the economy from the financial system's collapse, there are grave consequences from overreaching. Such intellectual blindness is about to have repercussions that Washington should have seen coming.

We wonder, then, what happens when inflation finally does set in. Will our politicians and policy makers have the courage to admit their mistakes and employ the necessary measures to pull the economy off the cliff of rampant inflation, or will we continue to be headstrong and stubborn? The question is critical because at the moment it seems that expediency rules the day. The great statesmen and -women who once fell on their swords are a vanishing breed, replaced by the slavish devotion to the 24-hour news cycle, with the need to maintain a political edge replacing the desire to do what's right not just for the moment but for the long term, regardless of its political consequences.

Herein lays a critical issue, because courage will be everything when tackling the inflation crisis. Ronald Reagan and Paul Volcker had that courage lo those 30 years ago when the nation found itself trapped in the suffocating burdens of soaring inflation, high unemployment, and gross domestic product contraction. They embarked on what was perhaps the boldest economic program of the century, comparable only to Franklin Delano Roosevelt's New Deal. Realizing that the nation could not keep going down the path of easy money, devastating taxes, and a withering dollar, they devised a highly unpopular political plan that temporarily pushed the country into a recession but simultaneously set the groundwork for the greatest peacetime recovery the nation had ever known.

The good news that began in the last chapter and continues here is that we believe strongly that Washington still has the necessary tools to bring the country back to prosperity. History teaches us that when leaders are willing to make difficult choices and keep their eye on the principles by which lasting economic growth is created, then America can overcome its looming crisis.

Our previous chapter, however, focused primarily on the negatives—stop devaluing the dollar; turn off the printing presses and halt the accompanying quantitative easing strategies; clamp down on public pension giveaways; and turn out the lights on the national spending spree. Those are all good things, for sure, but they do not address what we could call "positive" steps; in other words, things to put on the "What to Do" list rather than just fill up the "What Not to Do" list.

History provides many lessons of positive, proactive steps governments can take to halt the myriad problems on the near horizon. Yes, in case we haven't made this abundantly clear, when putting forth our case for a cure we will take a number of pages from the Reagan playbook. But we're also going to embark on a trip back to the Kennedy years and other places in between and around the horn of sound fiscal and monetary policies to prescribe the ailment for our staggering economy.

No, there will be no hair of the dog that bit us. The days of profligate spending, borrowing, and devaluing must cease. What we offer instead is a list of strategies—call them our Magnificent Seven, which is the amount of steps it will take to reverse this dreadful course. The quote cited at the beginning of this chapter, spoken by Charles Bronson in the 1960 classic when facing a gunfight of 30 against just the small group of our heroes, speaks to the difficult odds in making our plan work. But we, like Bronson's character, are optimists of a sort.

In some cases the recommendations are comparatively simple and should have been adopted long ago; elsewhere, we will endorse some measures that over a long haul would be antithetical to what would prevail in a perfect world. But it is important to recognize that this is no perfect world, and to close the onerous budget gap that has produced this insatiable need to borrow profusely will require considering some targeted, temporary means of taxation that will come at limited or no penalty for those most burdened already by the country's horrendously regressive tax structure.

Television preacher Joel Osteen is fond of saying that when an eagle encounters a storm, it flies over rather than through it. We hope the United States can be that eagle, but it will require a carefully charted course. Here are seven ways to get there.

Lower Income Tax Rates

Why is the prescription for budget deficits so often higher taxes? We see this scenario played out time and again in which a government gets itself in trouble with a budget shortfall and immediately decides the best way to generate revenue is by picking the pockets of society's primary wealth generators. Yet time and time again history teaches us that the only way to generate meaningful revenue that is nonpunitive to society is through lower, not higher, rates. Low tax rates encourage production and investment, reducing the burden for all of society through growth and free-flowing organic movement of currency. Higher taxes, meanwhile, discourage both production and consumption and actually generate higher inflation by pressuring both prices and wages to keep up. Lower taxes negate the need for artificial economic backstops like minimum wage laws and act as inflation-prevention measures by keeping the costs of goods and services low.

"Our true choice is not between tax reduction, on the one hand, and the avoidance of large federal deficits on the other," John F. Kennedy said during one of his most famous and eloquent speeches, delivered to the Economic Club of New York on December 14, 1962. "It is increasingly clear that no matter what party is in power, so long as our national security needs keep rising, an economy hampered by restrictive tax rates will never produce enough revenues to balance our budget just as it will never produce enough jobs or enough profits."

"In short, it is a paradoxical truth that tax rates are too high today and tax revenues are too low and the soundest way to raise the revenues in the long run is to cut the rates now," Kennedy continued, going on to bemoan a "chronic deficit of inertia" plaguing the economy because of its tax structure. "For on the strength of our free economy rests the hope of all free nations," he said in conclusion. "We shall not fail that hope—for free men and free nations must prosper and they must prevail."

JFK's words could have been spoken today just as easily as they were nearly 50 years ago. Economic history teaches us that when confronted with weakness the proper remedy is to grow, not suffocate, the economy. That doesn't happen by feeding the government and giving it more impetus to spend, but rather by allowing the powerful wheels of the free market to churn stronger and let the private sector works its wonders. Capitalism suffered a horrendous black eye during the collapse of the financial system. Its critics have had a field day casting aspersions on the free market as an abject failure that can live only with regulatory micromanagement. But as author Michael Medved points out in his wonderful book *The 5 Big Lies about American Business,* "Even at a time of financial hardship and menace, a celebration of the resilience and logic of democratic capitalism will make it easier to face the challenges ahead with inspiration rather than insecurity, and with gratitude above guilt."[2] We must keep these lessons as we make the decision to place progress above politics.

In a seminal but digestible—and monumentally important—study of the effects that lower taxes have on revenue growth, Daniel Mitchell of the Heritage Foundation examined three important junctures to see what cutting marginal tax rates had on the ability of government to generate revenue.[3] The results are compelling and unerring: The most effective way to growth is through reducing the tax burden.

Our first case in point is the 1920s. They weren't called the Roaring Twenties for nothing, and for how much we can deliberate the causes of the Depression, it certainly wasn't because the government wasn't generating enough revenue. The Harding and Coolidge administrations cut taxes through the decade and saw an increasing amount of receipts. Coolidge was wrong for not listening to Herbert Hoover about the perils of excessive stock market speculation, but his taxation policies were right on target.

Federal revenues rose from $719 million in 1921 (food stamps alone cost more than eight times that figure in 2010!) to $1.164 billion in 1928 as marginal tax rates dropped from 70 percent to less than 25 percent. At the same time, unemployment tumbled from 20 percent in 1921 to 3 percent at the end of the decade.[4] See the connection? While the relitigation of Great Depression causes is best left for another time, this prosperity may well have continued were it not for a series of policy blunders by Herbert Hoover and Franklin Delano Roosevelt after the stock market crash. The Twenties was a decade of great growth because the government understood its role; the following decade saw the system collapse because policy makers decided that short-term fixes like higher taxes and irrational trade barriers would be better than taking our medicine and sticking with pro-growth economic tenets.

The ridiculously high marginal tax rates of the Thirties would continue to plague the United States through the Roosevelt years, burdening society's best wealth producers with 90 percent tax rates that many found their way around by investing in tax-free securities and exploiting loopholes in the ever-growing tax code. It wasn't until John Kennedy took office in 1961 that a high-ranking government official decided it was time to attack the economic peril the country faced and slay the tax monster.

President Dwight Eisenhower and his Modern Republicanism programs brought the country a solid level of prosperity, uneven though it was. Eisenhower believed in the power of the market and the inherent fairness of capitalism and established a model that was as close to a "Goldilocks" economy as could be expected in America's postwar condition. But his quest to balance the budget was undermined by his refusal to cut taxes, and while his preference for the country to use long-term financing for its debts made some economic sense, the country remained in a deep philosophical disagreement over its debt and deficit issues. The average growth rate of 2.4 percent a year further underscored the notion that while Eisenhower's performance may have felt good, the economy still left much to be desired.

Seeking to eradicate the poverty that engulfed the South and some northeastern states, Kennedy embarked on a program that he justifiably felt would spread the wealth without artificially redistributing it. As such, he slashed the capital gains tax (a tactic Ronald Reagan would specifically back during his second run for the presidency in 1980) and attacked the rest of the rate structure. By the time the Kennedy years were over, the 90 percent top tax rate had been slashed to a still-high 70 percent.

The results were predictable: Federal tax revenues escalated from $94 billion in 1961 to $153 billion in 1968, a noninflation-adjusted gain of 62 percent and an inflation-adjusted rise of 33 percent.[5]

Reagan saw what Kennedy did and decided to give it a spin himself.

During the rabid inflation of the late 1970s, many Americans found themselves the subject of "bracket creep," which meant their nominal incomes were growing and pushing them into higher tax brackets even as their inflation-adjusted worth fell. Seeing the burden inflation was having on taxpayers sent Reagan into action. Though he raised some tax rates early in his first term—remember those two words again, "targeted" and "temporary"—once inflation was under control Reagan resumed cutting rates, and the federal coffers were the beneficiary.

We'll readily recognize that some of the Reagan Revolution was illusory and overly romanticized—poverty increased and so did the national debt—but his tax cuts were at the heart of a lasting and resounding period of prosperity. Total tax revenues nearly doubled during the Reagan years, and unemployment fell from 7 percent to 5.4 percent while inflation tumbled from 13.5 percent to 4.1 percent. Median income grew by $4,000 after experiencing no growth before he took office and a loss of nearly $1,500 after he left, an accomplishment that included no increase in the minimum wage (a topic we will address later in this chapter).

Ah, but what about that great disparity in the tax burden? Wasn't the little guy getting squeezed while deep pockets got deeper? Good questions. The record also will show that because lower taxes encourage investment and entrepreneurship, the rich also share an excessive amount of the burden during these times. According to the Mitchell study, which was first published in 1996 and refreshed in 2003, the tax cuts in the 1920s saw the rich (at that time those making the princely sum of $50,000 or better) increase their share of the burden from 44 percent in 1921 to 78.4 percent in 1928.[6]

In the Kennedy years, the results were much the same. As taxes fell, the share of the tax burden shouldered by top earners climbed 57 percent while the burden on lower wage earners rose just 11 percent.

The Reagan years followed a similar narrative, with the top 1 percent of earners paying 57.2 percent of the taxes by the end of his two terms, up from 48 percent, while the top 1 percent were now paying 27.5 percent of total taxes, compared to just 17.6 percent in 1981 when he took office.[7]

Mitchell rightly notes that lower taxes can't solve problems alone. Sensible austerity programs are important as well, and in Reagan's case it was particularly important that spiraling oil prices also were brought under control. But it's no coincidence that lower taxes have been accompanied by growing economies, lower inflation, and higher employment. Mitchell wrote:

> *Lower tax rates are important, but they are not the only critical issue. Both the level of government spending and where that money goes are very important. And even when looking only at tax policy, tax rates are just one piece of the puzzle. If certain types of income are subject to multiple layers of tax, as occurs in the current system, that problem cannot be solved by low rates. Similarly, a tax system with needless levels of complexity will impose heavy costs on the productive sector of the economy.*

No doubt taxes are a complicated issue and addressing marginal rates can only go so far. So let's go a bit further.

Reduce Corporate Income Tax Rates

Here is another nose-on-your-face obvious point that, again, is missed far too often in the course of charting tax policy. The United States is second highest in the world in corporate income taxes. We trail only . . . Japan.

We all remember Japan. That's the country that found itself in an economic bog in the 1990s similar to that of the United States in the following decade and decided one of the ways out was to embark on a futile revenue quest by taking it out of the hides of its corporations. We're reminded of that old antidrug commercial: This is your economy (picture of the United States) and this is your economy with crippling corporate income taxes (picture of Japan). Get the picture?

Japanese corporations in Tokyo are subject to a 40.7 percent tax rate, which after two decades has begun to strike the government as oppressive. In the summer of 2010 leaders there reluctantly began to recognize that it is folly to expect to grow an economy when your corporations cannot compete on a global level and attract foreign investment because taxes are simply too high. Of course, in Japan the problem is the opposite of what the United States is about to face with inflation. But economic growth is economic growth, and penalizing businesses for doing well is a deadly detour on the road to recovery.

The U.S. federal government over the past quarter-century has become increasingly addicted to the corporate net income tax as a revenue source. The tax is implemented on a graduating scale from 15 to 35 percent, but most companies pay the top rate as the profit ceiling is a relatively paltry $18.3 million. The levy now accounts for 2 percent of the total $14.5 trillion in national GDP.

But what if Congress gets creative and actually cuts corporate taxes? Political sentiment hasn't exactly been on the side of corporate America since the financial system collapsed and demonizing Wall Street became a favorite political blood sport. But history once again tells us that when the tax burden is eased on American businesses, receipts actually go up rather than down. This is borne out in a study from Oxford in 2006 and a raft of economic data not only in the United States but also in other countries belonging to the Organization for Economic Cooperation and Development.

The corporate net income tax is regressive on a number of fronts, both in simple percentage forms and in the way it actually represents double-taxation—once when the tax is actually paid and again when shareholders pay taxes on their profits. Like other taxes, it acts as a disincentive to growth and encourages chief financial officers to find ways to hide profits through tax shelters. It also makes foreign companies less likely to come to the United States; a recent study from the OECD found that for each 1 percent increase in corporate taxes, foreign investment falls by 3.7 percent.[8] Similarly, even U.S.-based companies are likely to push more and more of their operations overseas in an effort to avoid cumbersome domestic taxes.

"Lowering this tax would help American businesses compete with foreign corporations and unleash the entrepreneurial spirit of our workforce," said Euro Pacific Capital economist Michael Pento, one of a small breed in his profession trying to brace clients for the coming inflation onslaught. "In addition, lowering taxes on capital goods purchases and retained earnings would also encourage expansion projects, new hiring, and therefore general business development."[9]

A study from PricewaterhouseCoopers in February 2010 found that rolling back the corporate net income tax even to 30 percent would result in annual productivity growth of 0.4 percent.[10] A litany of other research accompanies this study. Among other findings, notable was a conclusion from the Joint Committee on Taxation that corporate taxes were the greatest inhibitors of growth among a variety of levies—even more than personal income and real estate, the latter long considered the ultimate regressive tax.

"Corporate income taxes appear to have the most negative effect on GDP per capita," the OECD said. "These findings suggest that a revenue-neutral growth-oriented tax reform would be to shift part of the revenue base towards recurrent property and consumption taxes and away from income taxes, especially corporate taxes." PricewaterhouseCoopers concluded: "The implication of this OECD research is that per dollar of revenue raised by the government, the corporate income tax, more than any other tax studied, imposes the greatest penalty on national economic growth."[11]

In other words, if you want to start shutting down the deficit-and-debt-spiral, one of the best ways to do it is to get off the back of corporate America.

One Exception: The VAT

The United States is virtually alone among industrialized nations in not implementing a value-added tax, and not without reason. Implemented recklessly, the VAT, as it is known, is susceptible to fraud and in fact can stimulate inflation rather than defeat it. Conservatives howl over this particular levy, which adds a charge on goods at each step of the production process. The Heritage Foundation's Curtis Dubay said the tax "would fail to close the exploding deficits" and said the economy would be better served if Congress would "end this cycle by simply restraining spending to historical levels and scrapping higher taxes, including the VAT."[12]

On some levels and in a more normal fiscal landscape, the argument is legitimate. But these, as we have said before, are not normal times. A $1.5 trillion budget deficit and a national debt more than 10 times that amount dictate that unusual measures need to be taken. Smart fiscal and monetary policies combined with manageable frugality measures as prescribed will go a long way toward closing both the debt and deficit gaps, but they won't fix everything. Some level of taxation will have to be involved, again keeping in mind our key words: targeted and temporary.

Paul Volcker has been a proponent of implementing a VAT, though the idea hasn't gone very far in the Obama administration as of this writing. A "sense of the Senate" vote taken in April 2010 found almost unanimous opposition to the idea, with 85 of the upper chamber's 100 members agreeing with a resolution calling the VAT "a massive tax increase that will cripple families on fixed income and only further push back America's economic recovery." Of course, it's hard to tell which recovery that might be—we're struggling to find one in our plodding U.S. economy. With Congress either unwilling or unable to start taking the scalpel to America's financial mess and bloated budget, it's a little late to start sermonizing about compassion for the common man.

"If at the end of the day we need to raise taxes, we should raise taxes," Volcker said in a speech to the New York Historical Society, after which the *Wall Street Journal* praised him for "candor" for "acknowledging that taxes on the rich can't begin to finance the levels of new spending that the current government has unleashed."[13] True, it was a bit of a left-handed compliment from the *Journal*'s editorial board, and it was accompanied by a fairly hysterical reaction common among those who view any tax as the mortal enemy of recovery. Critics worry that the United States will drift ever closer to becoming a European-style socialist state, and if the VAT is enacted recklessly those fears would have some traction. But reality is too difficult to ignore.

Spain's VAT, for instance, is now 18 percent, a level that is expected to raise 5 billion euros, or $6.16 billion. Yet Europe sets a poor example because in such countries the VAT has been implemented in a vacuum; that is, it is simply another tax foisted upon an overburdened citizenry.

Our proposal more closely reflects that of noted economist Arthur Laffer (coauthor, with Peter Tanous and Stephen Moore, of *The End of Prosperity*), who argues that the VAT should be implemented with corresponding cuts in income tax levels and spending.[14] Consumption taxes have the potential to be a complete game-changer, taking the burden away from those at the bottom end of the scale and placing it on those who can more afford to pay.

Finally, we also propose that a family of four making $60,000 a year or less get a $2,000-a-year tax break for the life of the VAT, adding another "T" to our critical formula of temporary and targeted: "tailored."

Of all the proposals put forth in this book, the VAT is perhaps the hardest for us to swallow. But we feel implemented the right way, it can help close the debt and deficits gap that will help trigger this crushing inflation threat.

Richard Bach once wrote, "There is no such thing as a problem without a gift for you in its hands."[15] So with the problem of the VAT, we also offer a gift.

How about a Holiday?

Austerity and tax cuts are two critical parts of the strategy to get the economy back on track and fight inflation. The third is growth. Without structural growth, achieved independently of the synthetic measures that have been used to prop up the economy for the past three years, the old foes that have dogged the United States will eventually win out. One of the best ways we can think of to achieve that growth is to give working men and women back the money the government has been pilfering from them.

Payroll taxes are as regressive as it gets, and the 6.2 percent levy, paid both by employers and employees, penalizes the working poor far more than rich people. Employers are discouraged from hiring at a time when it couldn't be needed more and employees see money they could use to support their families and foster growth handed indiscriminately to the government. But as unpopular and punitive as the tax is, politicians are loathe to touch it as the nearly $700 billion a year it generates helps fund the looming financial disaster known as Social Security. But in an economy that desperately needs growth and for consumers who badly need relief, a payroll tax holiday makes sense as an easy and fast way to provide help where it's needed the most without having to resort to more debt or to launch another artificial stimulus program.

There are some relatively painless ways to finance such relief. Indiana's Republican Gov. Mitch Daniels proposed spending cuts that include holding onto money not yet allocated through the Troubled Asset Relief Program, which bailed out the nation's banks, as well as pay cuts or freezes for federal employees. Economist Nouriel Roubini, who thinks the tax holiday should run as long as two years, has proposed allowing the tax cuts implemented by former President George W. Bush to expire to offset the lost revenue. Roubini's plans would effectively raise taxes on those earning over $200,000 immediately and for everybody else in two years. Cutting taxes by raising taxes doesn't seem to make much sense, but Roubini gets credit at least for thinking creatively when it comes to stimulus.

No such drastic measure is necessary. The payroll tax holiday would actually cost $20 billion less (according to 2009 revenue figures) than the TARP fund, which was used to bail out overleveraged and sometimes insolvent Wall Street banks. A working-class jump-start that didn't go toward pork-barrel spending (like the $780 billion stimulus program) would be welcomed both by consumers and businesses. The tax holiday deal that Congress and President Obama reached in late 2010 is a nice start, but it is only that. The holiday should be longer-term and more aggressive. The tax cut would benefit workers at the lower end of the scale, who are most likely to spend it and put it back into the economy, creating real demand and driving business. If a bailout is good enough for Wall Street, shouldn't it be good enough for Main Street, too? This is a populist proposal that works.

Extend the Retirement Age and Means Testing

Messing with senior citizens is about as dangerous as it gets in the political arena. But the notion that the government should start subsidizing its citizens' lifestyles when they turn 62, while a utopian ideal, simply doesn't make sense anymore.

There essentially are three ways to reform Social Security: (1) raise taxes; (2) cut benefits, or (3) alter the criteria we use to determine who gets benefits and when. Since the aforementioned payroll tax holiday negates the possibility of a tax increase, and because a cut in benefits is both politically infeasible and morally indefensible, the only logical course to pursue is reexamining the basis for receiving benefits.

Approved in 1935 and generating payouts two years later, Social Security accounts for 7 percent of gross domestic product and is the biggest beneficiary of all that money that comes out of your paycheck every week. It also helps keep 51 million Americans over the age of 62 out of poverty each month—though not far out. Benefits on average are less than $1,100 a month, and the fund is the constant subject of congressional scrutiny for, among other things, being a resource-draining quasi-Ponzi scheme that will come under intense pressure as the bulk of the baby boomer generation reaches retirement age. But it nonetheless has become part of the social compact, an agreement between the government and public that has spanned generations and at this point is essentially irrevocable.

Fully 36 million of Social Security recipients are over the age of 65, so at this point the idea of raising the age will apply to just under a third of total recipients—more as the baby boomers start coming on board. So it's an important part of the strategy to help reduce the debt and take some of the sting out of the inflation threat.

We're already well on our way toward raising the retirement age to collect full benefits, but even partial benefit recipients will now need to face higher requirements. Raising the retirement age to 68 for those who turn 62 in 2022 likely would cut the program's funding gap, currently as much as $12 trillion, by 29 percent. That's a great place to start, and it is part of a controversial proposal from the president's deficit-reduction panel to increase the age to 68 by 2050 and 69 by 2075—hardly draconian measures and accompanied by exceptions such as for people with hardships and those who work exceptionally demanding physical labor jobs.

Besides, when it was originally devised, Social Security wasn't meant to go to 62-year-olds. The program was targeted at those 65 or older and stayed that way until 1956, when women were allowed to collect at 62; men were added five years later. Moreover, it's not even financially beneficial to start collecting when reaching the initial age and partial benefits start to kick in. Those who wait until full retirement on average get greater benefits by waiting longer.

In all, hiking the retirement age is almost a no-brainer so long as sensible exceptions are kept in place.

Means testing for Social Security recipients is an equally divisive issue. The debate puts those who believe a certain level of income and assets should be taken into account when deciding eligibility for the program against those who feel public support will be undermined if not everyone is allowed to collect at the pre-ordained levels established in government formulas. More particularly, the debate is between those who believe Social Security cannot survive in its current form against those who believe any means necessary should be used for its march into perpetuity.

To be sure, severe cuts to Social Security are unjustified, and means-testing does, to an extent, amount to a bait-and-switch perpetrated against those who have paid into the program for all their lives. So let's take an elimination of benefits off the table right from the start. Instead, let's talk about people who obviously do not belong in any government entitlement programs, and work our way from there.

Means-testing already has been implemented in restricted forms, primarily through decisions that Social Security should not be completely tax-free. The Reagan administration began taxing 50 percent of Social Security benefits, and the Clinton administration hiked that level to 85 percent. Adjusting benefits to make sure those on lower incomes get proportionately higher benefits makes sense as we try to find ways to continue the program for those who truly are in need.

And here's a novel concept: How about giving wealthy Americans the chance to opt out? The financial advantages need to be studied more, but providing benefits to those who don't need them and really don't even want them seems a needless waste of taxpayer resources. While Social Security may be a smaller drag on the deficit than some of the bigger-ticket budgetary items, there is no doubt that reform is needed.

Eliminate the Minimum Wage

Either you're a capitalist or you're not. Either you believe in the ability of markets to determine fair pricing or you don't. Either you want to fundamentally change the way America does business or you don't. Take your pick, but the status quo just isn't working anymore. Our wage structure is antiquated and was implemented during a different time for the American worker, when abuses were commonplaces and sweatshops abounded. Wage controls have no place in an efficient free-market system.

The current minimum wage is $7.25, so a 40-hour work week at this rate will net you $290, or $15,080 a year. A married couple with one child living on that salary would be 18 percent below the federal poverty level. So let's agree that we're not talking about preserving working families and throwing starving children out in the streets. The minimum wage is used as a basement level to pay menial labor jobs, mostly to teenagers and part-time workers. Roughly one in 20 of the 72.6 million American workers paid hourly wages in 2009 was at the minimum wage or below. About half the 4 million or so in this category were teenagers, according to the Bureau of Labor Statistics. That's a steep decline from the 13 percent on the minimum wage in 1979, in the third year of the Jimmy Carter presidency, when inflation was soaring. Nearly 6 in 10 were in service-related industries, and the vast majority of these workers were part-time. Yet

Table 8.1 Inflation vs. Income in 2010: Inflation Is Winning

	May	June	July	August	September
Income Growth	0.4	0.0	0.2	0.4	–0.1
Inflation	2.02	1.05	1.24	1.15	1.14

this is the number that causes all the hue and cry from minimum-wage supporters who resist calls to eliminate a standard that does nothing but artificially and needlessly inflate the cost of doing business in the United States.

Of course these people will make all sorts of indignant claims that raising the minimum wage creates a rising tide that lifts all boats, pressuring the income of all Americans higher and raising the standard of living. But the facts do not bear out that position. Most recently, the minimum wage rose 70 cents an hour in 2009 from $6.55, and the carryover effects were underwhelming. While companies that use minimum wage workers now have to pay them 11 percent more, the wages for all Americans went nowhere. As of this book's writing, the five previous months' personal income gains were negligible, and actually negative when compared to the rate of inflation, which economists at the time were feverishly telling us didn't exist. See Table 8.1.

Cumbersome regulations and taxes add even more to the cost of creating employment in the United States. Eliminating some of the silly job-killing regulations along with taking the austerity measures prescribed here will go a long way to fostering true growth in the economy. Americans have seen millions of jobs slip away overseas because the country simply cannot compete with foreign workers, particularly on costs. Propping up the wage structure with inefficient impediments only adds to the problem.

Raise the Bar for Education

Perhaps the most esoteric of our recommendations is a call for revamping our nation's education system, and it also may be the most important. If we are ever to restore American competitiveness by eliminating debts and deficits, it has to start at the foundation of our system.

By now most of us know the statistics and how dreadful things stack up for the United States compared to the rest of the world. We're all familiar with the fact that the U.S. education system, burdened by decades of neglect and well-intentioned but ultimately futile programs, ranks behind those of many other industrialized nations by any number of metrics. (We're 33rd, for instance, in reading, 27th in math, and 22nd in science, according to data from the Organization for Economic Cooperation and Development.) How can we seriously expect to compete on the global stage when our educational system is in such disarray? American education is a story of an overburdened system, top-heavy with administration and saddled by uncontrolled costs and not enough attention to providing students with the skill sets they need in a changing world.

Yet there is one area where American education system is competitive: its unparalleled college and university system. The top five universities in the world—Harvard, California Institute of Technology, Massachusetts Institute of Technology, Stanford, and Princeton—are all in the United States, according to the Times Higher Education survey, produced in London.[16] The United States has 7 of the top 10 and 15 of the top 20. So how did that happen if the K through 12 system is in such disarray (ranked 48th in the world, according to the World Economic Forum)?

One word: competition.

The United States' university system is great because it has to be. Harvard has to step up its game or risk losing students (and the fat endowments they'll provide upon entering the top rungs of the workplace) to Yale. Stanford has to remain sharp or its students might choose UCLA instead. See how that works? It's the same thing in business. Company A, which makes widgets, has to keep costs low and quality high or watch its customers buy Company B's better, cheaper widgets. This is the very basis of our system. As we stated a few paragraphs ago, either we're capitalists or we're not.

If this system works so well in our business climate and at the collegiate level, why all the commotion over applying it to our public schools? The omnipotent teachers unions might be able to provide that answer. The National Education Association and its many locals throughout the country have been battling with all their breath efforts to impinge on their turf. The unions feel threatened by any type of school choice, be it vouchers, charter schools, or any other option that might take resources away from our mediocre school system and divert it to programs that are making real strides in preparing our children to compete.

It's time to stop making excuses for why public schools shouldn't face the same type of competition as private industry—competition that has helped strengthen our economy and has made American companies far more competitive in the global marketplace.

School vouchers, which provide financial aid to students wanting to attend private schools, have been particularly effective at achieving this goal. The dozen or so programs implemented thus far in the United States have consistently shown that financial aid to attend private schools has provided opportunities to disadvantaged students that they would not have received otherwise. A comprehensive study undertaken by Brigham Young University in 2008 found that "parents are much more satisfied with their child's school if they have used a voucher to choose it. We know, through the assistance of a substantial body of rigorous experimental studies, that the effect of vouchers on student achievement tends to be positive."[17] The study notes that the benefits of vouchers remain somewhat inconclusive—primarily because we don't know what will happen when voucher programs are extended to broader segments of the student population other than the disadvantaged. This is a legitimate caveat and one that ought to get the ear of policy markers everywhere: Voucher programs have shown extremely promising results so far, so it's high time to start expanding the programs to more students.

But school choice shouldn't be limited to vouchers. Grassroots organizations and excellent corporations are making efforts across the country to establish charter schools, and those efforts should be supported through tax incentives and the proper allocation of public resources so these institutions can offer choice to parents and students. The use of vouchers, credit deductions, and rebates are helping more than 190,000 American students attend private or charter schools. That's a good start, but it's not enough.

We save this recommendation for last because quite simply unless the United States strengthens its resolve to rebuild our educational system on a fundamental, structural level, all the other financial maneuvers—be they tax incentives or increases, austerity measures, relaxing of regulations, or the rest of the batch—won't make a lick of difference.

No Easy Fix

It's important finally to note that fixing the debt and deficits problem can't be done by any one or two measures alone. Too much austerity could kill economic growth; tax cuts without corresponding spending cuts will exacerbate the problem. Indeed, the prognosis is grim but the remedy is available. It's up to us where we go from here.

Chapter 9

Investing in a Time of Crisis

This is not an investment book designed to show you how to invest all of your hard-earned assets. One of us (Tanous) has written several investment books that go into some detail on investing and building a portfolio. But we feel strongly that, given our backgrounds in investment management and financial journalism, we cannot in good conscience tell you about the financial crises we see coming without offering guidance on how to protect your assets from the perils that lie ahead. We are not going to recommend specific stocks or mutual funds but rather share with you thoughts on how traditional asset allocation may need to be revised given the stock market meltdown in 2008 and early 2009 and the outlook for inflation in our foreseeable future.

We believe that we are at a major turning point in how we must look at investing for our financial well-being. For many years, investment management has been guided by the principles that derive from what is known as Modern Portfolio Theory (MPT). The theory, developed by Harry Markowitz, a Nobel laureate from the University of Chicago, holds that diversification is key to successful portfolio management. The idea is that different types of assets behave differently at different times, so the best way to even out your investment returns is to intelligently diversify your assets and make sure you are investing over the long term.

Or so the theory goes.

Honestly, while MPT does work, the real issue is in the definition of *long term*. No doubt you have heard the quote from renowned economist John Maynard Keynes, who, when discussing the long term, said: "In the long term we are all dead."[1] So let's add a dose of realism to the notion of investing for the long term.

Common stocks have been the basic building block of all investment portfolios for decades. There's a good reason for that. Stocks have been the best performing asset class in American history. Another fact that adds to our confidence in the stock market is that we have a history of stock market performance that goes back 90 years. Over that 90-year period, stocks have returned (from both capital gains and dividends) more than 9 percent a year.

We wish we could end the discussion right here, but most of us don't invest for 90 years and need to look at other time periods for returns on stocks. Indeed, there have been periods of very high returns in stocks, and other periods of long droughts when, if we had only known, it would have been better to avoid the stock market for many years. We don't have to go back all that far for examples of droughts. The most recent example was the 10-year period that ended in December 2008. During the preceding decade, stocks had *negative* returns—you lost money in the stock market if you simply owned an index fund for that 10-year period.

It Is All about Risk

If there is a single powerful attribute that envelops everything we do, it is the concept of risk. We consider this subject so important that we have devoted a chapter to it a bit later on. Here's a simple question: Why do we ever take chances with our hard-earned money? Why do we risk losing some or all of it by assuming the risk of the stock market? We could put our money in government bonds or a bank certificate of deposit and sleep well at night, knowing our money was secure.

The answer—which you likely already know—is that we assume risk to get a better return on our money. If we want to earn, say, 10 percent on our money, we know that the bank or the government will not (in normal times) pay us that kind of risk-free return. If we want to earn more, we have to assume more risk. One reason we try to earn higher returns is that inflation may well wipe out some of the purchasing power of our savings. We are predicting serious inflation in the near future. So to keep ahead, we need to earn higher returns than those ordinarily available from those "safe" investments in banks or government bonds.

We spend billions of dollars annually in pursuit of the goal of making money. All of the investment firms, all of the investment advisors, all of the investment books and literature, all of the prattling experts on CNBC, Bloomberg, and Fox Business TV channels, and all of the investment newsletters and investment experts have one thing in common: They are going to tell us how to make money and not lose it in the process.

We know better.

One important way to look at the risk and reward parameters between stocks and other assets is to examine the long-term relationship between the stock market and 10-year Treasury bonds. At the outset, let us make the point that the 10-year bond is "riskless" only if you keep it to maturity, at which time the bond is repaid and you get your invested money back. The 10-year bond can fluctuate with interest rates and, should interest rates rise, the principal amount of your bond could be worth less money in the interim period until your bond matures and you get paid back. But for comparison purposes, using the 10-year bond is the practical and safe alternative to stocks for most long-term investors.

Over time, stocks have offered a higher return than bonds. This is normal, and the reason is simply that you get rewarded for taking risk. The amount by which stocks return more than bonds is known as the "risk premium." That means that the extra amount you earn by owning stocks is the compensation you earned for taking the risk that your stocks might go down (and lose money) rather than go up.

Over the years, investors have expected to earn about 5 percent more in stocks than safe bonds as compensation for the risk they were taking with stocks, and that 5 percent extra return was the risk premium.

In Chapter 12, we will take an in-depth look at our knowledge of risk, how it has evolved over the ages, and where we are today.

Have We Succeeded as Investors in the Stock Market?

We pointed out earlier that for the last 90 years, stock market returns have averaged about 9 percent a year, a very good return. Please remember that we are talking here about returns for the stock market as a whole, not for any individual money manager or mutual fund guru who might beat the stock market averages. Indeed, those nice folks who work at brokerage firms are eager to point out that, on average, the stock market rises two-thirds of the time on an annual basis. Again, these are pretty good odds if you are deciding whether or not to risk your money in the stock market.

But it doesn't tell the whole story.

A stock market gain of as little as 1 percent in any given year makes that year a "winner." We need to keep in mind that we always have choices for our money. We could leave it in the bank, buy bonds, buy real estate, buy gold, or buy an array of assets other than stocks.

Now let's go back to comparing stock market returns to the 10-year Treasury note. Most stock market investors diversify the types of investment in their portfolios. This process is known as asset allocation. Typically, an investor will have, as a minimum, stocks and bonds in his portfolio, with the bonds serving to reduce the risk and volatility of the portfolio as a whole. The idea is that the stocks will provide most of the growth and, when the stock market is sliding, the bonds will mitigate the damage, since the bonds will decline little if at all.

That's the theory, and most investors have been doing just that for a long time.

Let's look at some sobering facts. Here is the most basic question that all investors must ask: over the last 5, 10, 15, or 20 years, did I

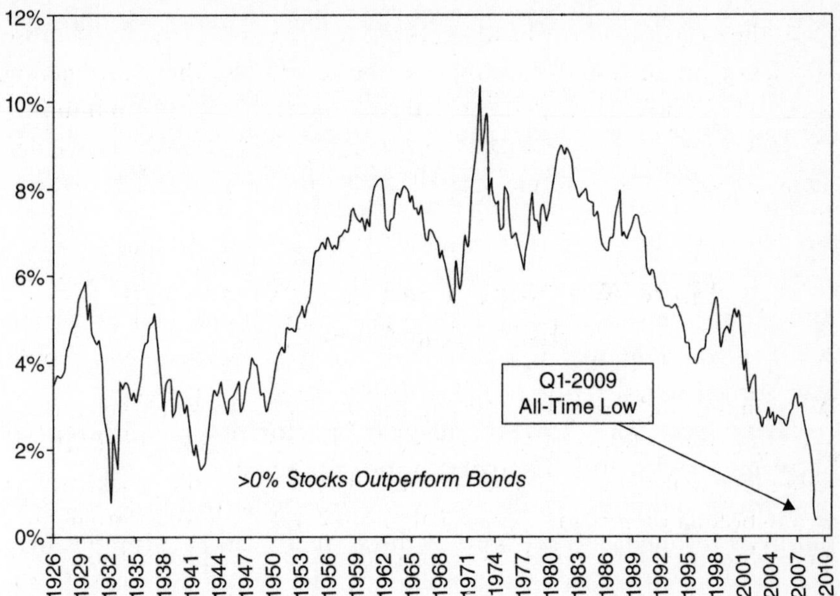

Figure 9.1 Stock/Bond Performance Differential,* 40-Year Trailing Total Return ACR

* S&P 500 vs.10 Year Tteasuries

Source: The Leuthold Group, LLC, 2009.

get compensated for the risk I took when I bought stocks instead of bonds?

The answer to this question will surprise and perhaps even shock you as we look at data from the bottom of the market in March 2009.

Around the bottom of the market after the huge market decline in 2008 and early 2009, the total return (capital appreciation plus dividends) of the S&P 500, as of March 31, 2009, trailed the total return of the 10-year Treasury bond for the last *1-, 3-, 5-, 10-, 15-, 20-, and 25*–year periods![2] Look at Figure 9.1, which shows the difference in annual compounded returns (ACR) between the stock market (S&P 500) and the 10-year Treasury bond. The wavering line shows by how much stocks have returned more than the 10-year bond over the years. You can see that at the end of March 2009, the bottom of the stock market after the 2008–2009 crash, the trailing annualized excess return of stocks over the T-bond was at an historic low. The actual number, over the trailing 40 years, is a return for stocks of just 0.3 percent over bonds. Forty years! It is true that the market has recovered nicely since March 2009, but these statistics are sobering indeed.

Think about this extraordinary turn of events. Assume that over the past 40 years you had invested in stocks and endured the 1973–1974 stock market decline; the 1987 stock market crash; the Internet bubble; 9/11 and a market that was closed for a week and in chaos for a period thereafter; the combined 40 percent decline in stock prices in 2000, 2001, and 2002; and the meltdown of 2008–2009. And your compensation for taking that risk? At the end of March 2009, it was a meager 0.3 percent annually more than you would have earned in safe 10-year Treasury bonds.

That was the lowest 40-year performance differential between stocks and Treasury bonds in history.

Perhaps more realistically, many investors who had bought stocks and lived through one or more of those stock market calamities may well have given up along the way and sold out of the market at a significant loss. Institutions invest for 40 years; individuals don't. However, we must pay attention to the risk/reward benefit of owning stocks, and the current long-term statistics are just plain frightening.

Should I Still Own Stocks?

After spending several pages describing what a lousy investment stocks have been over the past decade and more, we now have to tell you that you should still own stocks. The reality is that there is nothing better to ensure long-term dollar growth. We have just described a period, ending in March 2009, that statistically marked the worst period in American investment history for long-term investors. It was a moment in time, to be sure, but a miserable moment. The stock market recovered sharply starting in April 2009 and the S&P 500 rose 23.5 percent for the full year 2009 while the NASDAQ index rose 43.9 percent.

There is always the temptation to time the market, but it rarely works. An investor might consider our dire outlook for the world of finance and decide that now would be a really bad time to own stocks, and he may be right. The problem is that we just don't know how the stock market will behave in the short term. Perfect example: In September 2010 the U.S. stock market jumped about 9 percent. No one predicted it, nor could they have done so. A 9-percent return is something most of us would be happy to earn in an entire year, and the stock market handed it to investors on a silver platter in just one month. The point is that you had to own stocks to take advantage of it. Timing the market is for amateurs. The professionals know better.

What has changed is that instead of the old traditional investment formula of 60 percent stocks and 40 percent bonds, the asset allocation must today reflect the elevated risk, and it must also change to incorporate new asset classes that we may not have considered previously. These new asset classes will be just what we need to grow our wealth in times of crises.

So here's the plan. Your personal investment advisor will tell you how much of your assets to put in stocks and bonds. We want to describe to you in some detail why it is very important that you have a meaningful part of your assets in two specific inflation-protecting assets that we discuss in the next chapters.

One additional point about bonds: In the inflationary environment we see coming, there is no place for long-term bonds in an investment portfolio. Long-term bonds with interest coupons of, say, 4 percent will be worth considerably less than par should interest rates soar to perhaps 8 percent or higher. Bonds are supposed to dampen volatility in an investment portfolio, not contribute to it. So for the bond portion of most portfolios, we recommend Treasury Inflation-Protected Securities, known as TIPS. These bonds adjust for inflation, so the lower yield an investor gets early on can be more than compensated for by the increase in the principal amount of the bond the government will contribute if inflation comes. TIPS have problems of their own since they may not reflect the full impact of inflation, but some protection is better than none.

Investing in an Inflationary Environment

If serious inflation comes to our shores, as we believe it must, investment attitudes will change, perhaps dramatically. Indeed, when inflation is present, we tend to look at investments differently. When you hold that $100 bill in front of you, what does it represent? Most of the time it represents a currency backed by the United States and a purchasing power that is known and reliable. But when inflation sets in, people start to look at that bill as what it really is: a piece of paper. If your purchasing power declines through inflation, that $100 bill does look different because it no longer buys as much as it used to.

In this environment, our attitudes change quickly. We emotionally shift our attention from paper assets to real assets. And what is real? In its simplest form, they are the things that you can hold and touch that have some intrinsic value. Obvious examples are real estate, food, precious metals, and oil. We believe that every investment portfolio should have a dedicated allocation to inflation-protection assets. Among the safest such investments are TIPS. These Treasury bonds adjust for inflation. Every six months, Uncle Sam adds to the principal amount of your bonds an amount equal to the amount of inflation. Other inflation-protection assets are more volatile and bear more risk. Most of them are commodities. We will focus on only two of these that we believe belong in just about every portfolio designed for long-term growth.

The types of investments we favor are those characterized as real assets. Real assets are distinguished from other commodities in that they are not manmade. These real assets include energy, raw land, precious metals, base metals, and potable water. From an investment point of view, we want to concentrate on two assets that share the following characteristics:

- Increasing demand
- Diminishing supply
- Limited substitutes

Our two candidates: oil and gold. We discuss both in the coming chapters.

Chapter 10

Gold Still Good

Of all the countless maxims that populate the investment marketplace, the theory that gold is best positioned to help investors avoid the currency-eroding effects of inflation is one of the most treasured. While some may dispute whether gold actually is the "ultimate" inflation protection, history certainly shows it's at least in the top three. Gold not only looks pretty and makes nice jewelry, but it also has tended to hold its value when currency is being depreciated.

Let's look at what is on the horizon: Debt defaults in the European Union combined with the rising costs of debt financing in the United States will produce soaring interest rates. At the same time, developing economies demand the commodities we use in our daily lives, sending prices soaring. Amid it all, investors will need a place to take cover. That's an easy case for gold.

There are any number of reasons why gold works as a way to protect portfolios when the cost of living starts soaring, but the primary reason is that inflation reduces confidence in currency so investors need a place that can work as a *store* of money. It is important to remember that one of the key tenets of gold is that it has only marginal intrinsic value other than its function to make necklaces, rings, and fancy watches. Gold is not a commodity that can be consumed. Gold is not a currency in of itself, so it can't be used to pay for things. Gold is not part of a manufacturing process, nor can it be used like other metals such as palladium to make catalytic converters for cars. Gold merely *is*—that is to say it has stood the test of time, through the 2,600 years since old King Croesus began issuing gold coins that actually could be redeemed for value.

So What Is Value?

But what is *value?* Some economists like to consider value the product of an acronym: DUST. The D is for demand. Do people want gold? Yes they do. Whether it be to store in bullion, to wear in jewelry or to diversify their investment portfolios, they want the shiny yellow metal. The U is for utility. Is gold usable? Well, we just talked about the sad fact for gold that it has little use. But that doesn't mean it has no use, and if investors really do consider the metal to be the ultimate inflation hedge, then indeed it does have some utility. Besides, the world is full of products that can be described as "useless." Beer, for example, has no health or nutrition benefits but is one of the most beloved products in the world. So let's agree that beer has utility, if for nothing else than it is something to enjoy on a hot summer day at a ballpark while contemplating the size of your next gold purchase.

The S is for scarcity. While gold's value isn't always related to its availability, we know that we can't simply walk to the gold mine down the street and pick some out of a pile. So it does have a level of scarcity, a quality that is magnified every year as the amount of gold actually pulled out of the earth decreases but the demand for it increases. Finally, the T is for transferability. Can one person or entity give gold to another person or entity? Of course. Whether it be through buying gold bars, coins, jewelry, or through more esoteric means, such as the purchase of shares in the popular exchange-traded fund SPDR Gold Trust (GLD), gold can be delivered from one person or institution to another. So gold, contrary to what you might hear from the anti–gold bugs, does have "value" as defined through the DUST acronym.

The question we must answer, then, is not whether gold has value but why we want to buy gold when currency depreciates and prices rise. Here's a simple fact: In recent times, gold has almost always risen against falling currencies. That in itself tells you that if the United States continues with policies that either intentionally or unintentionally cause the dollar to lose its value, gold will at least help you achieve the proverbial return of capital if not the return on capital.

Some, in fact, have argued that gold is not simply a hedge against inflation but in fact is a hedge against uncertainty in tumultuous times. The price of gold made a steady trek upward when the first traces of the financial crisis hit in early 2008, peaking at just over $1,000 before falling below $900 in April 2009.[1] Then a funny thing happened. The Federal Reserve began in earnest a program known as quantitative easing. Some people like to call it money-printing, but regardless of any sobriquets quantitative easing has been an enormous boon for gold investors. Quantitative easing, or QE as it is more familiarly called, works like this: The Fed doesn't physically print new money, but it does credit its account with a certain amount of dollars (a "quantitative" target), which it uses to buy various securities—Treasuries, mortgage debt, car loans, whatever the central bank believes will help create the flow of money in the economy. In turn, the Fed's purchases provide capital to those holding the securities, hopefully triggering a virtuous cycle in which the money is plowed back into the economy through loans and other investments. The "easing" part means the Fed is facilitating the flow of money in hopes of generating liquidity and thus economic growth.

Why Is This So Good for Gold?

Why is this so good for gold? Primarily all that QE makes the dollar lose its value due to simple laws of supply and demand. The greater the quantity of something the less value it has, generally speaking. (Remember the S in our DUST model. Greater scarcity means greater value.) Investors, then, turn to gold as a store for their paper money, which they don't want to see lose value. You see, then, why we encourage gold holdings as one of the most fundamental investment choices during times of great uncertainty and particularly in an inflationary environment.

This, of course, is not a new strategy. Investors have turned to gold in similar economic times. In fact, as this book was being written gold was near its all-time nominal high of $1,424 an ounce but well below its inflation-adjusted high. That was achieved when gold hit $875 an ounce, which translates into $2,320 in today's U.S. currency. We're guessing that you'd be able to provide an accurate timetable of when that occurred—in January 1980, when inflation stood at 13.9 percent, just below the 14.76 percent peak it would hit in March of that year. The November 2010 price range of gold in the $1,400 neighborhood would be just $527.45 in 1980 dollars, so we have a ways to go yet.[2] That's even more good news for gold: If you think the current price sounds high, history shows that the metal can go much higher until it reaches a breaking point.

If you asked the average gold investor for reasons to own the metal, you'd probably get half a dozen answers. But we'd like to focus on three that provide ample justification for having a strong component of gold, as well as gold-related companies and exchange-traded funds, in your balanced investor portfolio.

Let's emphasize one point first: Gold is a great inflation hedge, but it's not the only inflation hedge. In this section of the book, we discuss some other highly viable options, such as Treasury Inflation Protected Securities as well as real estate and real estate investment trusts (REITs). Let's focus on gold as inflation protection for now.

Three Good Gold Reasons

Our top three reasons for gold start with its ability to serve as a surrogate for paper money, a point touched on earlier in our discussion of quantitative easing. For many years, the United States and most of the industrialized economies indexed their currencies to gold. You might know it better as the *gold standard,* a term nowadays used wistfully by monetarists when recounting the olden days when money actually was backed by something other than the full faith and credit of the debt- and deficit-laden government issuing same. (You'll sometimes hear the term *fiat currency* used to describe the state of affairs nowadays, and it's simply a reference to money that is backed only by government guarantees and no actual assets such as gold.) The gold standard officially ended in 1971 when President Richard M. Nixon did away with the last vestiges of the Bretton Woods currency system, which had been agreed to in July 1944. The United States simply began printing too much money to pay for the Vietnam War and its other overseas entanglements and it no longer was feasible to peg the currency to a certain level of gold pricing. The "Nixon shock" began an age in which the U.S. dollar became the world's reserve currency but nonetheless had no actual asset backing.

The second reason people buy gold is to make jewelry. China and India are the global leaders in this regard, so it may not be any accident that the two governments' central banks have been some of the greatest purchasers of the metal over the past several years. In addition to inflation fears, the Chinese and Indian economies are two of the fastest-growing in the world, so consumers there will demand more gold. Interestingly, Chinese citizens up until just a few years ago were forbidden to buy gold, from an edict more than half a century ago at the hands of dictator Mao Zedong. Consumers essentially are playing a game of catch-up, enjoying the new luxury. In addition to China and India, Turkey and various Middle Eastern nations have been buying gold for jewelry, accounting for 68 percent of the global demand. It also is suspected, though there is only scant data to back this up, that sovereign wealth funds have been big gold buyers. It is known that China Investment Corp., the nation's largest sovereign wealth fund, has been buying gold through the previously mentioned GLD exchange-traded fund. Investors favor exchange-traded funds (ETFs) because they are composed like mutual funds but trade like stocks. As of late November, the GLD fund held 1,285 metric tons of gold.

The final primary reason people buy gold is plainly and simply as an investment. Many investors believe that stress in government or in the capital markets will always create uncertainty, and it is during those

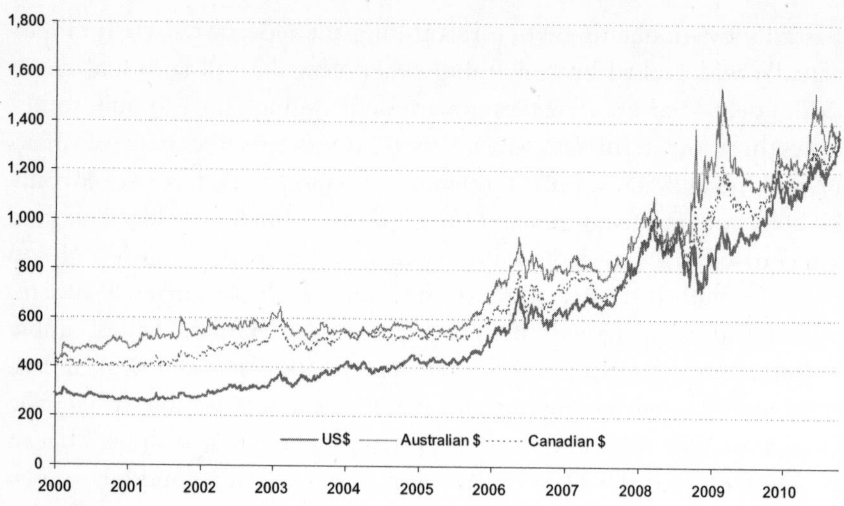

Figure 10.1 Spot Gold Price in Major Producer Currencies
SOURCE: IHS Global Insight.

times that gold becomes an excellent store of money providing a respectable return. During the uncertain times in the last five years of this century's first decade, gold gained against the U.S. dollar, yen, euro, British pound, and the Swiss franc. (See Figure 10.1.)

Global investors continue to recognize the value in gold. Central banks in Bangladesh, Sri Lanka, Thailand, and Saudi Arabia have been slowly making purchases, which in turn triggers citizens of the tiny countries to get in on the action.

Our focus here, though, is on the importance of gold as protection against inflation. A highly useful study from the World Gold Council shows how money creation, which we monetarists believe is the key ingredient to inflation, is correlated to the price of gold. As the Fed has continued to expand its balance sheet (approaching $3 trillion as of the most recent count), the flow of money as measured through the general metrics of M1 and M2 has steadily progressed higher. (M1, which we will use here, is a measure of all currency and coins held by the public, along with checking accounts, negotiable orders of withdrawal and all other demand money. M2 includes M1 along with other time-related deposits, savings accounts, and individual money market accounts.)

M1 grew roughly 6 percent through the first 10 months of 2010. The World Gold Council found that for each 1 percent change in M1, gold gains 0.9 percent six months later. In the meantime, as this growth in the monetary base was happening, gold soared a stratospheric 21 percent! (Have no fear, though; this growth is not as bubblicious as it sounds, as we will soon show.)

Thus, the council concluded:

> *Our analysis suggests, firstly that gold is a leading indicator of velocity and therefore inflation, and secondly that despite a large output gap around the world and anemic economic recovery, investors are justified in their concern that quantitative easing policies resulting in rapid money supply growth will eventually lead to an increase in the velocity of money and of inflation.*[3]

Might an organization called the World Gold Council be suspected of bias? Perhaps, but the council's conclusions are based not on opinions but on statistically sound regression models using mathematical computations that we shall not get into for our book. Suffice it to say we are convinced that the historical trends are clear that when more money is being injected into the economy, inflation is sure to follow. As stated earlier, this is simple supply and demand.

But Is It Bubblicious?

The final question we shall want to address is the perfectly legitimate concern of whether gold is in a bubble. Such a stratospheric rise in an asset that takes at least some of its cues from monetary policy expectations rather than fundamentals should be examined at least on suspicions of bubble behavior. We can confidently say, though, that with inflation and geopolitical uncertainties firmly entrenched on the horizon, demand from foreign nations strong, and the need for gold as a surrogate currency strongly in place, the possibility that gold is in a bubble and thus due for a breakdown is next to nil.

We previously discussed how gold, though at a high in pure dollar, or nominal, value is far from its inflation-adjusted peak, which occurred during the very worst of stagflation of the late 1970s and early 1980s. Not only is gold not at its true historical peak, but it is not even close. This is important for two reasons: First, based on simple analysis, investors are not near their peak of fear that would only drive them further into the metaphorical arms of gold as a safety investment tool. Second, when gold did reach its inflation-adjusted high, it was indeed in a bubble and due for a collapse, which occurred as inflation ebbed, confidence returned in the economy, and the dollar strengthened.

So how is this time different?

For this argument we shall use the M2 money measure. Remember, M2 is M1 plus time-related deposits, savings, and money market accounts held by individuals rather than large institutions. The measure is a good way to determine just how much money really is available to be pumped into the economy, and it also serves as a yardstick to determine whether gold has entered that dangerous bubble territory, which made casualties of the dot-com and real estate industries.

What is a "bubble"? Many people incorrectly assume that just because the price of something has gone parabolic that it is making a bubble. This is not necessarily the case, at least on the upside. Sometimes we see huge increases in prices simply because something had heretofore been grossly undervalued—sort of an inverse bubble. These circumstances often follow a bubble. Think about oil in 2009. As global paranoia increased about whether the world's financial system was going to collapse completely and the U.S. dollar was getting crushed, crude oil jumped to $147 a barrel. In retrospect, it appears a silly thing, thinking that American consumers, already strapped over the decline of their housing values and facing the shriveling of their retirement accounts as the stock market crumbled, could somehow afford to pay $4 a gallon for gas. The market, realizing that oil had gotten into a massively speculative bubble, then turned the other way, sending crude below $40 a barrel and cutting that $4-a-gallon gas price in half. As we found out, neither price was correct. But as the market gyrated and consumers reacted accordingly, price discovery was achieved. We found that oil between $70 and $90 a barrel was that elusive Goldilocks price—not too hot, not too cold, but just right. Sure, we'd all like to go back to gas below a dollar a gallon, but the marketplace knows that it is not the correct price based on supply and demand.

Instead of some arbitrary gut feeling of knowing when a bubble is forming, we like a definition that New York Fed President William C. Dudley espoused in an April 7, 2010, speech to the Economic Club of New York:

> *Turning to the first issue of whether there are asset bubbles, I am going to be a bit of a heretic and argue that there is little doubt that asset bubbles exist and that they occur fairly frequently. By an asset bubble, I mean price increases (or declines) that become unmoored from fundamental valuations.*

Dudley made his observation knowing that people who believe in the perfect marketplace—the "efficient markets hypothesis" as he would point out—would disavow the existence of bubbles because if an asset price got too frothy the market would automatically correct. History tells us this is not true, at least not in an immediate sense, so even though we think the market does ultimately correct bubbles, it often is powerless to prevent them from occurring and doing a substantial amount of damage. Fighting the Fed is treacherous business, and the insistence on creating easy money in the marketplace is prone to continue to cause bubbles.

So, again, how do we know that gold's price isn't in bubble territory? The easy answer would be to go back to our January 1980 reference to find that by inflation-adjusted standards gold is nowhere near its peak. But that reasoning is insufficient and bordering on intuitive rather than deductive. That time period, though, does provide another quite useful reference point.

At that time, the price of gold compared to the M2 money supply measure was much higher than the historical mean of 12. As the economic team of Ronald Reagan, Paul Volcker, and Arthur Laffer moved in to control inflation by tightening the money supply, gold was bound to tumble. Gold and money supply should follow a fairly consistent path together, and if gold veers much in one direction or the other, we'll know that the formation of a bubble, or an inverse bubble, is not far behind. Look again at Figure 10.1. We can clearly see that the trajectory of gold to money supply is nowhere near the dangers of an asset bubble.

The World Gold Council has done other excellent work in ferreting out whether gold truly is in a bubble.

One metric it has used is comparing the quarterly annual rolling returns of gold to expectations. Statisticians use standard deviations to measure such occurrences, each unit being a proscribed level of movement away from the median, or most common, result. One standard deviation, for instance, would be seen as outside the realm of normal expectations but still within reason. Two standard deviations would be considered a borderline normal result. Anything beyond two would indicate an aberration—for the purposes of this study a sign that a bubble was forming.

As confirmed in our look at the 1980 bubble, the returns were outside the two-sigma, or standard deviation, realm. But the council's research found no other similar events since. While a comparable look at housing, technology, and Japanese stocks during the same period all displayed bubble characteristics, gold did not.

Finally, the council compared the rise in gold prices to those of the Standard & Poor's 500, oil, and gold's sister metal, silver. Ratios compared to each asset were found to be consistent with historical norms. "Therefore," the council concluded, "in examining gold price appreciation relative to global equity markets and tangible assets like oil and silver, we find that gold's price remains consistent with long-run average levels."

Looking forward, it's not hard to see that monetary policy is going to be a friend to gold. Even if you discount every other concept put forward here, it is impossible to argue with the statements from the Federal Reserve itself that it is nowhere near a policy that would constrict the flow of money. Even if the Fed calls off its quantitative easing program, which it well could do sometime around the release of this book, the $3 trillion of assets it already has pumped into the economy is going nowhere. Even as QE ends, the Fed will have to navigate perhaps its most difficult waters yet, namely figuring out how it is going to return all of the assets it owns—unwind its balance sheet, as some people describe the process—without creating the huge inflows of capital into the economy that will be one of the key drivers of inflation. As this happens, gold will have nowhere to go but up.

A Piece of the Action

The final question we address here is "What is the best way to invest in gold?" There are many avenues investors can use to take advantage of an asset that easily should hit $2,000 an ounce by 2015 and likely will have a clear path to $3,000 by the end of the decade. Each option has its benefits and drawbacks.

The most basic way is to buy physical gold—coins, bars, or other items made of pure gold. Once limited to huge bars or coins like Krugerrands, gold now can be purchased in virtually any size, from fractions of an ounce up to large gold bars. Generally speaking, when purchasing gold like this, bigger is almost always better. Shipping and packaging of gold is quite costly, so an economy of scale makes buying small amounts generally less cost effective. The primary drawback to buying gold like this is what you do with it once it's purchased. Storage is expensive, so your physical holdings probably should be limited.

The second, and most popular, way to buy gold is through exchange-traded funds. The most popular gold ETF by trading volume is the SPDR Gold Shares Trust (NYSE: GLD), which holds actual gold and closely tracks its price. The iShares COMEX Gold Trust Fund (NYSE: IAU) also tracks bullion's price. ETFs are a popular investment vehicle because they are composed like mutual funds but trade like stocks. In the case of gold ETFs, they also help reduce volatility and can help investors avoid some of the other burdens of gold, particularly storage. They also offer some protection against volatility as might be experienced from short-term traders who work with gold futures contracts.

A third way to get a piece of the gold action is through companies that will benefit from the rise in prices yet to come. In particular, we look at gold mining companies whose business should perk up both from the increased demand for gold and what likely will be an at least somewhat diminishing supply. An easy way for investors to take advantage here is through ETFs that follow the gold miners. The Market Vectors Gold Miners fund (GDX) is popular and tracks the AMEX Gold Miners index. Barrick Gold Corp. is its largest holding.

We advocate gold as important portfolio protection for the storm clouds we see clearly ahead. To be sure, gold is not the only protection against inflation, and the rest of this section of the book explores the various other options investors have for protection. But based on the current trajectory of the economy, with rising interest rates and soaring inflation on the horizon, gold promises return without the risk. An essay by economist Michael Pento deftly explored the relationship between real interest rates—the yield on the 10-year Treasury note minus the rate of inflation—and found that when that number turns negative, gold becomes a fabulous investment tool.[4] That's because gold's returns, unlike many other asset classes, are based not on interest rates but rather on market rates. So when inflation destroys the value of money in real terms, gold just keeps on moving higher and shields investors from such treacherous climates.

Chapter 11

The World Still Runs on Oil

There's an old expression: Nothing is certain except death and taxes. At the risk of engaging in epistemic arrogance, may we add another element to the list of certainties: the price of oil? We'll back off that certainty a bit somewhat later, but the point is simply that the supply and demand equation for oil is about as pure as it gets and its anticipated future price rise fits very nicely with our thesis about inflation. So why isn't this point so obvious? For one, the recent history of the price of oil is quite volatile, so our belief in an upward trajectory for future oil prices is mitigated by short-term price swings.

Let's start with a look at the long-term history of crude oil prices through 2008 in Figure 11.1. The chart shows the history of oil prices in both real (inflation-adjusted) prices and nominal prices. The line at the bottom is the nominal price of oil since 1861, and it shows a virtual flat line for over a century. You can follow our little history of oil prices as you read on by occasionally looking back at the chart to see the price changes we describe. The oil situation got much more interesting and intense during the Carter administration and the 1973

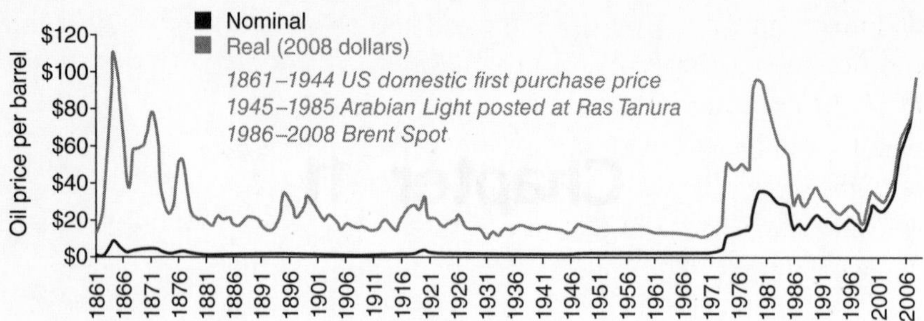

Figure 11.1 Crude Oil Price History
SOURCE: Energy Information Administration.

oil crisis. If you are old enough to remember the oil crisis, you will surely not need a reminder of what it was like. In October 1973, the members of the Organization of Petroleum Exporting Countries (OPEC), or more accurately the Arab members of OPEC, imposed an embargo on shipments of oil to the United States in response to the U.S. decision to help Israel during the Yom Kippur war between Israel and her Arab neighbors.

On October 16, 1973, OPEC raised the posted price of oil by 70 percent, to $5.11 a barrel. The embargo, which amounted to a gradual cut in production until OPEC's political objectives were met, came the next day. The United States continued its aid to Israel even in the face of the embargo, and later that month most Arab oil producers cut all shipments to the United States. The total embargo soon included all of Western Europe.[1]

The effect of the embargo in the United States was immediate and drastic. The price of oil went up 400 percent almost instantly, from $3 a barrel before the embargo to $12 a few months after it started. Everyone old enough to remember will recall the endless lines at service stations where cars lined up for hours as millions of Americans topped off their gas tanks. It was a decidedly unpleasant moment in American history.

In the aftermath of the oil embargo and the recession that followed, the stock market declined by 40 percent in 1973 and 1974, the worst two-year decline since the depression.

In early 1974, Secretary of State Henry Kissinger negotiated an Israeli troop withdrawal from parts of the Sinai. The beginning of diplomatic initiatives by the United States to address the Middle East conflict caused the Arab oil producers to lift the embargo in March 1974. Much damage had already been done, however, and the future of oil would never be the same thereafter. The 1970s saw a period of high inflation in the United States with consumer goods prices and interest rates rising at an alarming rate. The prime lending rate reached 21 percent by 1980 while the U.S. Treasury was issuing long-term bonds with an unheard of interest rate of 14 percent.

In the 1980s, the economy recovered, interest rates and inflation subsided, and the price of oil stabilized. Americans were driving smaller cars and using less fuel. OPEC and the rest of the world recognized that the supply of oil was finite, and production quotas were set lower. Efforts were undertaken to stabilize the price of oil. Then an unexpected phenomenon occurred: While the OPEC members were held to a specific production quota, some of them got greedy and cheated! The cheaters produced and sold more crude than they were allowed to in order to raise more revenue. Saudi Arabia played the good guy role and simply cut back its production to maintain the world price even while other countries cheated. However, by 1986 the Saudis made a simple decision: "No more Mr. Nice Guy." Since many other countries were cheating and getting richer in the process, the Saudis, who were by far the world's largest oil producers, decided to teach them a lesson. They increased production by 250 percent, flooded the market with oil, and sent the world price plummeting to $10 a barrel. Big cars were back in fashion!

The calm in the price of oil was again broken in 1990 when the United States invaded Kuwait to save the small but important oil-producing nation from an attack by Saddam Hussein and his Iraqi army. A war between leading producers of oil had a predictable effect on the oil price, and prices did indeed spike. After the short war was over, oil prices again declined and by 1994 had reached an inflation-adjusted price level that was actually lower than the $10 a barrel price of the early 1970s.

The price of oil fluctuated thereafter through various political and economic events, including the 1997–1998 Asian crisis and, of course, 9/11. By the time we were well into the new millennium, a new phenomenon began to take hold—the realization that perhaps there was not enough oil on the planet to satisfy the growing demand, especially the demand from the two fastest growing and most populous countries in the world: China and India.

So here's the problem. The following paragraph from a paper one of us (Tanous) wrote on oil in 2006 is still relevant today:

> *According to the* Energy Economist Newsletter, *"In mid-2002, there was over 6 million barrels per day of excess production capacity, but by mid-2003 the excess was below 2 million. During much of 2004 and 2005 the spare capacity to produce oil was less than one million barrels per day. A million barrels per day of spare capacity is just 1% of world oil demand, not enough spare capacity to cover an interruption of supply from almost any OPEC producer. In a world that consumes 85 million barrels per day of petroleum products, that adds a significant risk premium to crude oil price.*[2]

Now the world still consumes about 85 million barrels of oil a day, but changes they are a-comin'! Much the same as a few years ago, the supply/demand equation for oil remains tight. At any given time there are only 1 million or 2 million barrels a day of spare capacity. We'll talk about some other implications of that statistic a bit later. For now, Figure 11.2 shows the number of vehicles per thousand in various parts of the world back in 2006.

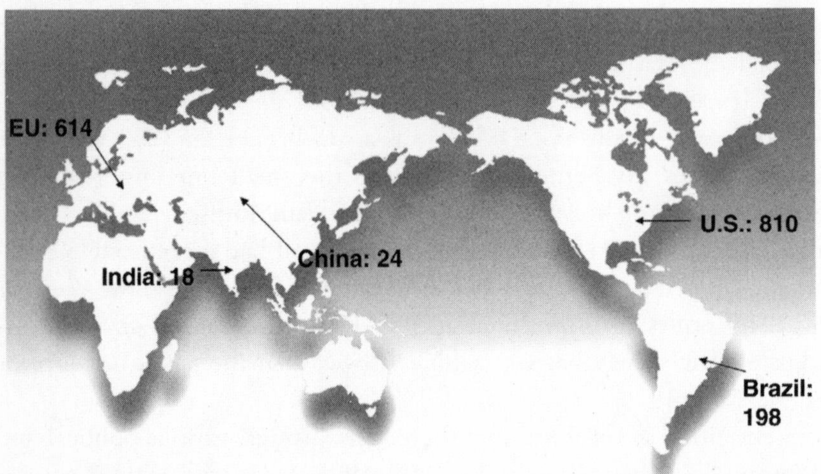

Figure 11.2 Number of Motor Vehicles per Thousand People
SOURCE: World Bank Development Indicators Report 2006.

No one will be surprised that the United States, with 810 vehicles per thousand inhabitants, is by far the most profligate user of vehicles in the world. Europe is next with 614 vehicles per thousand, and you can see from the chart how the rest of the world stacks up. Now pay attention to India and China. These are the largest countries in the world, each with over 1 billion inhabitants. They are also among the fastest growing countries in the world. With rising wealth come rising standards of living. Here again, it's no surprise that one of the first things that an economically emerging family craves is an automobile. And it is happening in these countries at a very rapid pace. Auto sales in China are expected to increase 25 percent in 2010. China has already surpassed the United States as the number one automobile-producing nation. India's sales will grow about 13 percent, not as fast as China's because India has been raising interest rates to slow demand. This torrid demand pace may well slow, but does anyone have any doubts that China and India's number of vehicles per thousand population will double very soon? When it does, those countries will, in the case of China, have 48 vehicles per thousand population and India will have 36 per thousand. These are still puny numbers compared to the rest of the world. Look again at the figures for the other nations.

The major point here comes into focus when you realize that China currently consumes 7.5 million barrels of oil day and India 2.8 million barrels. When their consumption doubles from these very low numbers, they will be adding 10 million barrels a day in consumption to the world's total. That doesn't include the natural growth in demand from the rest of the world. Recall that the world today consumes 85 million barrels a day and the world produces about the same amount. Where will the oil come from to meet an extra 10 million barrels a day of demand? That is equivalent to the entire production of Saudi Arabia, the largest oil producer in the world and the source of one fifth the world's oil supply. It is unlikely that we will discover another Saudi Arabia to meet the new demand.

It is certainly true that alternative fuels will progress and gradually increase their share of the market. But this is a very slow process and gasoline-powered engines will be with us in quantity for several decades. The supply of oil simply will not keep up. You know what happens when demand exceeds supply: The price goes up.

Peak Oil

There has been a lot of talk about peak oil and, in fact, a great deal of debate over the subject. First, let's define peak oil. It is the point when the maximum rate of global petroleum production is reached, after which the rate of production enters terminal decline. Peak oil shouldn't be confused with oil depletion; peak oil is the point of maximum production while depletion refers to a period of falling reserves and supply. Basically, there will come a time when the world runs out of oil. The clock will start running when we reach peak oil and production begins to decline. The endless debate is about when that peak oil point will be reached.

The International Energy Agency (IEA) estimated that we reached peak oil several years ago, a rather gloomy assessment. Even the most optimistic prognosticators believe that peak oil is no more than a decade ahead of us, while others believe the entire argument is silly since technology will always keep us ahead of rising demand. The World Energy Resources Program of the U.S. Geological Survey produces the official estimates of world oil resources for the U.S. government. It estimates remaining world oil reserves at about 1 trillion (1,000 billion) barrels, which would mean that world oil reserves would be exhausted in 50 years at the current rate of consumption.

The fact is that we will indeed run out of oil at some point. For all practical purposes, however, the peak oil debate is not something we need to concern ourselves with today unless we like going to old men's clubs, sitting in overstuffed leather chairs, lighting a cigar, and harrumphing with colleagues about peak oil and the end of the world. What we need to worry about is the supply and demand for oil, and on that score we believe demand wins.

For this and another reason we will mention shortly, we believe that all portfolios should have some allocation to oil. Why doesn't everyone own oil? The fact remains that it is still a commodity and it is subject to economic forces. Its most recent history is testimony to that fact. In the summer of 2008, oil reached a dizzying price of $145 a barrel, and then the recession hit with a vengeance. The price of oil plummeted to less than $40 six months later. Few investors can stomach that kind of volatility. However, we believe in investing in oil for the long term because the market provides an almost inevitable case of higher demand and lower supply. It may well be volatile in the short run, as are all commodities, but the long-term outlook is very clear to us. The price of oil will rise.

Finally, another wild card in oil investing is not pleasant, but it is worthy of mention: war and civil unrest in oil-producing countries.

The Scary Scenarios

In today's political environment, we can hardly ignore the effect on oil prices of political, terrorist, or other problems in a major oil-producing country. Indeed, in February 2011, a wave of civil unrest created havoc in Egypt, Tunisia, and Libya and the price of oil spiked. Without digressing into a political analysis, it is safe to point out that most of the problems that have to do with civil unrest and potential or actual hostilities happen disproportionately in oil-producing countries. It is also true that given the tight supplies in the market for oil worldwide, the slightest threat to a major oil-producing country creates considerable economic anxiety and invariably results in sharply higher prices for oil. Think about the following countries, which all conjure up fears of war or civil unrest: Iraq, Iran, Saudi Arabia, Kuwait, Nigeria, Venezuela, Mexico.

And, of course, they are all major oil producers.

Now, we are not suggesting that you own oil and start wishing for armed conflicts or revolutions, but if they occur, and depending on the severity and the location, the stock market will react negatively and oil will spike upward. At the very least, owning oil in such cases will be an excellent investment diversifier.

Owning Oil

Your personal investment advisor can tell you how to profit from the rise in price of oil. Here are some additional points we would like to add. First, *do not* buy the oil exchange-traded fund, USO. For technical reasons we won't go into here, it is a poor way to own the commodity and might not track the price of oil in a rising market. An easier way to profit from the rise in the price of oil is to own shares in large and small oil companies and oil service companies. One large mutual fund that invests accordingly is the Vanguard Energy Fund.

Finally, let's sum up the oil investment strategy. Oil is almost certain over the long term to be in short supply—as nations grow there will be more demand for oil than there is supply. That suggests that the price will go up. Unfortunately, oil is still a commodity and commodities react to economic cycles. We saw this in 2008 when oil reached a high near $145 a barrel and collapsed to under $40 before beginning to recover. Our parting message is to own oil for the long term but only if you are able to handle sometimes severe short-term swings in the price.

Chapter 12

Understanding the Investment Risks We Face

Throughout our discussion of investments in this book, we have often talked about the subject of risk and how it permeates just about everything we do in life. Indeed, risk is everywhere. Every time we cross a street we risk getting hit by the proverbial bus. When we take a new job, or decide to get another academic degree, we take a risk. The risks we want to discuss here are those that we face every time we make an investment decision. When we buy a stock, bond, mutual fund, or gold coin, we are assuming some risk. Unless you are a short seller, we all share a desire that our investments will appreciate in value. We have consciously or subconsciously made a judgment on the odds that we will succeed. Obviously, we believe the odds are in our favor or we would not have made the investment.

And how good are we at understanding and quantifying risk? This subject has intrigued academics for centuries. It is a subject well worth examining. In this chapter, we take you on a brief history of risk through the work of the many legendary figures who have studied it.

We look at how the understanding of risk has evolved and where we are today.

When you flip a coin, what are the odds it will come up heads? Everyone knows the answer to that one: 50 percent. So if you flip a coin 100 times, tails will come up 50 times and heads will come up 50 times, right? Most of us also know the answer to that question, too: It might work out that way or it might not. If you try the experiment yourself, you'll end up with many different results. Heads may come up 60 times and tails 40 times in one case. Or tails might come up 58 times and heads 42 times. The greater the number of flips, though, the greater the chance that the end result will be close to 50/50.

What if in the course of our little experiment heads comes up eight times in a row? What are the chances heads will come up on the ninth toss? The answer, of course, is still 50/50. The coin is not blessed with a memory. It doesn't know that it came up heads eight times in a row. The odds on the next flip are still 50/50.

We are talking about coin flipping to introduce the subject of probability. Interestingly, probability theory was slow to get off the ground throughout history. The ancient Greeks didn't have much use for it, nor was much time spent on it in the Renaissance. Yet every insurance company must deal in probability theory to price a life insurance policy or any other kind of insurance. After all, the company needs to have some idea of the odds that the insured will die and it will have to pay his heirs the insured amount.

Probability is a function of mathematics, so most of the work done in this field is credited to great mathematicians. For our purposes, we zero in on mathematicians whose works were concerned with stock price movements rather than the chances of a monsoon, or life expectancy, or games of chance, even though in many cases the theories are related.

A Brief, Selective History of Risk

We believe that one of the most important reasons investors lost so much money in the stock market in 2008 and early 2009 is that none of us truly understood the risks we were taking with our investments. In order to gain a fuller understanding of the risks of investing, we explore the history of how we got here. The way we look at stock market risk today has its origins hundreds of years ago, although we pick up the story in Germany in the latter half of the 18th century. We follow the logical path of how the financial community analyzed risk back then to how we do it today and we explore the contributions of a number of Nobel Prize winners in economics. Alas, as you will soon see, this is how we got into so much trouble. Read on.

Carl Friedrich Gauss: One of the Greatest Mathematicians of His Time

We begin our journey with Carl Friedrich Gauss, who was born in Braunschweig, Germany, in 1777. Gauss was born into a poor, working-class family, but his genius quickly became apparent. At age 3, computing the results in his head, he reportedly corrected a column of numbers his father was working on. Through a series of fellowships, and with the encouragement of his mother, Gauss landed at the University of Gottingen and soon began to attract attention for his elegant and important mathematical discoveries. His book, *Disquistiones Arithmeticae,* which he wrote in Latin, made significant contributions to number theory. But it is Gauss's work on distributions of statistics, resulting in the Gaussian bell curve, that is of most interest to us in the analysis of risk in the stock market.[1]

Although Gauss's contributions to mathematics were monumental, his life was a difficult one. Mathematicians generally are not gregarious, outgoing people, and Friederich Gauss was no exception. Gauss married young, but his first wife, Johanna, died prematurely in 1809. One of his six children with Johanna died shortly thereafter, and Gauss went into a deep depression. He subsequently remarried, to his late wife's best friend, but she died in 1831 after a long illness. The broken old man was cared for thereafter by one of his daughters until his death in 1855.

Friederich Gauss's difficult personal life did not impede his monumental achievements, and his fame spread all over Europe. Indeed, it was reported at the time that in 1807, French troops approached

Gauss's town of Gottingen but stopped short under orders from their commander, Napoleon, who spared the city because one of the greatest mathematicians in history lived there.

Among Gauss's greatest achievements is his use of the bell curve. Somewhat counterintuitively, the bell curve is used not to determine accuracy, but rather to determine error, and by how much. (The bell curve was originally developed by a French mathematician, Abraham de Moivre, about 80 years earlier.) When we invest in stocks, we might expect to earn a 10 percent return over the years, but since we can't forecast that return accurately, what we really want to know is how far off our return might be from the 10 percent we expect. That is what we mean by "error." Now we are into the study of probability. For example, you are planning a vacation trip to Hawaii next month. What are the chances it will rain a lot during your trip? If we take a bus trip to Chicago in July, what are the chances the bus might crash? Would we be safer in an airplane? What are the chances of a stock market crash? The bell curve and Gauss offered an answer.

Even if you've never heard of the term *bell curve,* you may remember talking to your fellow students in high school or college about an exam that was going to be "graded on the curve." Figure 12.1 shows what it looked like. Grading on the curve simply meant that the professor was not going to assign a specific grade for each exam based on how many right answers each kid got. Instead, since the test was particularly tough and since most of the kids did poorly, he might decide to use the curve, which meant distributing the grades around a mean, or an average. So even if all of the results were lousy, the

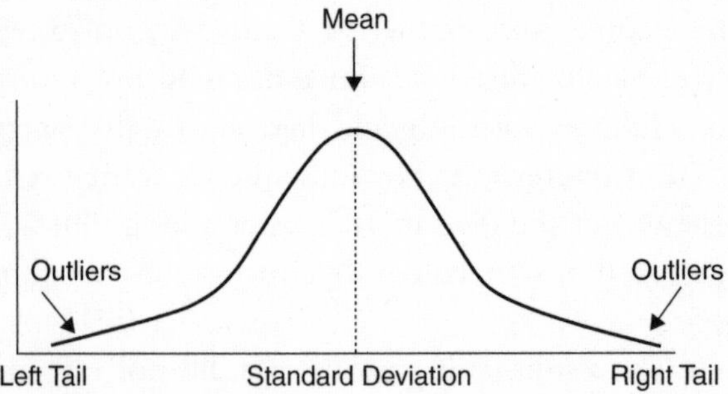

Figure 12.1 The Bell Curve
SOURCE: Lepercq Lynx Investment Advisory.

teacher would give an average grade, say a C+, to the ones that were average for the entire group of papers, and then distribute the rest of the grades around that average grade, or mean. The ones who were better than the average would get a higher grade, and the ones who were worse would get a lower grade. That meant that even if you didn't do well on the exam, but if you did better than everyone else, you got an A.

What the bell curve does is show the distribution of a number of phenomena or events. Let's talk about stocks. If you consider buying a high-tech company stock that has a range of prices over the last five years between $4 and $125 a share, we would all agree that that particular stock is volatile. On the other hand, a different stock, perhaps that of a public utility, only fluctuated between $20 and $30 over the same period. Clearly, the utility stock is much less volatile than the high-tech stock. The changes are measured statistically by something called "standard deviation." The majority of stocks don't move up or down that much, and those that move around the least represent 68 percent of the total sample of stocks. That 68 percent group is said to be within one standard deviation of the mean. Ninety-five percent of the stocks are within two standard deviations, and 98 percent are within three standard deviations. Using this scale, you can easily see that standard deviations of greater than three are rare events indeed.

Consider another type of distribution: average male heights. Assume that the average height of men in the United States is 5′8″ with a standard deviation of 2 inches. That means that 68 percent of men are between 5′6″ and 5′10″ tall. Ninety-five percent of men are between 5′4″ and 6 feet tall; that's the two standard deviation measure. Now we get into rarer territory: three standard deviations. At this level, the men range between "shorties" at 5′2″ and tall fellows of 6′2″. The distributions continue on both ends of the bell curve with increasingly rarer results, from little people to NBA centers.

The distribution of probabilities was an important contribution to the study of risk. From this curve we derived the term "outlier," which refers to the extremes of the bell curve on each side. If we look at investment returns of various managers or mutual funds and compare them to the return of the stock market, we generally find that most of the fund and manager returns are close to the mean, which is the return of the stock market. At the tails, the outliers on the right are those managers or funds that had much higher returns than did the stock market, and these are rare indeed. On the left tail, we have the returns of managers and funds that were significantly lower than the return of the stock market. Nobody cares or talks about them.

First Major Work on Probability

In our brief journey through the history of risk, we now focus on Louis Bachelier, whose doctoral thesis, "Théorie de la Spéculation," is generally considered to be the first major work on the theory of probability in the field of finance and markets. This work became the foundation on which a later generation of economists would build their theories of investing and risk. Unfortunately, Bachelier's fame and recognition came long after his death. When his doctoral thesis was presented to the judges at the Université de Paris in 1900, the panel was not impressed. Bachelier's early schooling had been undistinguished, and the jury knew that. Moreover, his chosen thesis topic of speculation on the trading of options on French government bonds on the Paris Bourse, the French stock exchange, was not universally recognized by the judges as an appropriate topic for serious academic study. When the judges convened, Bachelier received a *mention honorable* for his work, a grade one notch below the one that would have ensured his snagging a choice position on the teaching faculty of a major French university. So the 30-year-old Bachelier spent more than two decades in lesser academic positions as a lecturer and high school teacher before finally landing a permanent professorship at the Université de BesanÇon.[2]

Bachelier's thesis was first an attempt to understand price movements in the market. There are many factors that determine the price of a stock or bond (Bachelier was primarily concerned with bonds and options on bonds). The general direction of the market is one factor, as are inflation expectations and the current prospects for the issuer of the bond, as well as a slew of other factors that might affect the price at any moment. In fact, even the conclusions derived from these factors differ so that there are those who think the price might go up (buyers) and those who think it might go down (sellers). All of this uncertainty makes it impossible to devise a mathematical formula to forecast price movements. But, as Bachelier significantly pointed out, there are enough data to establish the *probability* of market moves based on the state of the market at any given instant.

Bachelier was fascinated by the seemingly random price movements on the bond exchange, and he studied them for patterns. His first conclusion was that the market was a "fair game"; no one investor knew any more than any other investor. In that case, the chances of buying a French bond and watching its price go up rather than down was 50/50, the same odds as a coin flip. Bachelier observed that when the price of a bond moved significantly, up or down, it was always possible to rationalize the price movement after the fact. The company had a bad year, the chief financial officer snatched a pile of the company's cash and absconded to Rio with his girlfriend, interest rates were rising, and so on. All of the possible scenarios served to explain the price movement *ex post facto*. But, of course, this was not possible to do *ex ante*, or before these facts came out. So what change caused the price to move? New information.

To some readers this explanation will start to sound familiar. It is the basis of the efficient market theory later devised by Eugene Fama and his colleagues at the University of Chicago. But early in the 20th century, Monsieur Bachelier was already onto something, and he didn't stop there. He plotted all of the price changes of various bonds over several months. Displayed on a graph, the price data produced a bell curve, where the small changes in daily prices, those that occurred most of the time, were clustered around the center of the bell curve, and the very largest changes, up or down, were at the tails. Herr Gauss was smiling in his grave.

But Bachelier was not satisfied. He knew, of course, that future prices of bonds or stocks could not be predicted accurately, but as a mathematician, his goal was to formulate *probabilities* of the direction of future price movements. A century earlier, another great French mathematician, Jean Baptiste Fourier, had developed equations to demonstrate the way heat spreads and Bachelier had studied these formulas in school. Bachelier adopted some of Fourier's formulas to calculate the probability of bond price movements. A Scottish botanist, Robert Brown, conducted similar studies of pollen particles circulating in water in a seemingly random pattern. The challenge was to determine whether the particles were a form of life. Brown concluded that they were not alive and that the movement of the particles was indeed random, much as would be the trajectory of a big beach ball bouncing over the crowd at a Beach Boys concert propelled by dozens of raised hands hitting the ball as it approached. The only reasonable conclusion is that the movement of the particles, and of the beach ball, is random. The study of this effect became known as "Brownian motion." This phenomenon applied not only to the movement of particles and to the diffusion of heat, but also to the seemingly random movement of stock and bond prices.

Bachelier took these findings a step further and developed mathematical equations to determine the probability that an investor, or speculator, would earn a profit if he bought options or futures contracts, on the Paris Bourse. His formulations were uncannily accurate. A few years later, in 1905, Albert Einstein developed his own equations, which were very similar to Bachelier's; Einstein, however, set out to confirm the existence of atoms and molecules and in the process became four times as famous.

Students of stock market history will see where all this leads. In later years, the notion of the efficient market, where prices reflect all known information, the random walk theory, which suggests that stock price changes are random in the absence of any new information, and the Black-Scholes option pricing model all derive in one way or another from the work of Louis Bachelier.

Harry Markowitz and Modern Portfolio Theory

In the 1940s, when Harry Markowitz was finishing high school in his native Chicago, he developed an interest in the study of philosophy and physics. After earning his undergraduate degree at the University of Chicago, he decided to stay there and pursue advanced degrees in economics. He studied with Milton Friedman, perhaps the greatest economist of our times and the leader of what was soon to be called the Chicago School of Economics. George Shultz, who was dean of the business school, would subsequently become U.S. secretary of state. Arthur Laffer, of Laffer Curve fame, who was also at the University of Chicago at the time, would follow Shultz to Washington. Friedman would become the first of a line of Nobel Prize winners from the University of Chicago. Years later, in 1990, Harry Markowitz earned the Nobel Prize in Economics.[3]

At a time when most stock market theories concentrated on the expected return on investment, Markowitz focused on the risk investors assumed when they bought stocks. In 1952, the *Journal of Finance* published a short article, "Portfolio Selection," by a graduate student in his mid-twenties, Harry Markowitz. With this paper were born the principles embodied into what was later to be called Modern Portfolio Theory (MPT), which is still very much practiced and revered. In essence, Markowitz took the position that an investor should consider not just each stock he owned separately, but rather the concept of the portfolio, which should be looked at quite differently from a collection of individual holdings.

In its simplest form, MPT is about investment return, investment risk, and investment diversification. Most of us realize intuitively that when we invest in the stock market we assume some degree of risk. That makes sense. We all know that stocks can go down and lose money as well as go up and make a profit for the shareholders. If we could get the same return by investing in a safe bank CD, why would we bother with the stock market? Unlike the very long odds of gambling on a lottery ticket or a slot machine, the only reason investors are willing to assume the risk of investing in stocks is that they expect a higher return for assuming that risk. What Harry Markowitz taught is that by diversifying our various investments across different types of stocks, bonds, and other investments, we can *reduce* our risk and enhance our returns. It was a great idea, to be sure.

Think for a moment about the concept of diversification. What's the first expression that comes into your mind? Our bet is: Don't put all your eggs in one basket. What exactly is the message conveyed by this common expression? Literally, if you are skipping along the path to Grandma's house with the basket in hand and you happened to slip and fall, all of the eggs in your basket would be broken. That's covariance—if the basket falls, all the eggs would break. Had the load been "diversified" among the other relatives going to brunch at

Grandma's, say, each relative carrying one egg, a single slip-up would destroy only one egg rather than all of them. There is no covariance among baskets being carried along different paths. Their fates are not intertwined.

In the case of a stock portfolio, this means we must try to own stocks that don't tend to act in the same manner. If we buy a basket full of tech stocks, for example, they have a lot of covariance, just like 10 eggs in one basket. If tech stocks go down, it is likely that all of our stocks will go down, much as all of the eggs will get broken if we and our basket suffer a nasty tumble. So we diversify our portfolio of stocks by buying stocks of different companies in different industries that tend not to behave in lockstep. Likewise, 10 eggs in 10 separate baskets is a lot less risky than 10 eggs in 1 basket. The eggs in the 10 baskets have no covariance. The 10 eggs in 1 basket have a lot of covariance! For example, if a report comes out that retail sales declined, you won't be surprised if most of the retail stocks decline in the aftermath. So you don't want to own a concentration of retail stocks. That's 10 eggs in 1 basket!

This may sound fairly obvious, but the notion of diversification and risk was an earth-shattering discovery in the field of finance. Markowitz went on to write a book, *Portfolio Selection: Efficient Diversification of Investment* (John Wiley & Sons, 1959), which was essentially his PhD thesis. The book was published in 1959, and the history of investment selection changed forever.

In theory, when an investor buys any stock in the market, he assumes investment risk in the form of stock market risk. The stock market moves up and down in unpredictable fashion, so an investor who wants to make money by buying a stock that he hopes will go up must assume the risk that it might go down. Diversification helps reduce that risk by encouraging the investor to buy many stocks so that the risk is spread out over his entire portfolio. But Markowitz points out that for the diversification to be useful, it has to be the right kind of diversification. For example, if you bought not 1 but 10 tech stocks today, you would not have diversified properly because tech stocks tend to behave as a group, going up and down in synch as the market views the outlook for that sector either positively or negatively. In technical terms, Markowitz suggests that a portfolio should not have stocks with high covariances among themselves.

Covariance is a term to describe assets, in this example stocks, that move up or down together. Tech stocks have a high covariance because they do, in fact, tend to move up and down in price as a group. To minimize risk, a portfolio should have stocks with low covariance. In addition to our tech stocks, we might want to own some consumer goods companies, like Procter & Gamble, which will not be affected by the same economic or market factors as the tech stocks. In short, to achieve a desirable portfolio, we seek to reduce covariance.

Markowitz referred to the desired collection of assets as an efficient portfolio. An efficient portfolio should provide the highest return for the amount of stock market risk an investor is willing to take. Not all investors have the same investment objective or the same tolerance for risk, so one size won't fit all. Markowitz realized this and developed the formulas for calculating the ideal portfolio composition, among stocks, bonds, and any other measurable asset class, for a given level of expected return and assumed risk the investor was prepared to take. This concept he called the efficient frontier. If this phrase sounds familiar, it is likely that you have an investment advisor who prepared a portfolio of assets for you using precisely the concept developed by Markowitz and still very much in use today. Indeed, it is more widely used today than ever before because the calculations required are formidable. In Harry Markowitz's day, computers were primitive and slow and it took days to perform the thousands of calculations required to produce an efficient frontier for a given portfolio. In many cases, computer time was available only in the middle of the night and even then at a high cost. Remember that getting this right first required calculating the possible ranges of each asset's price performance. Then you calculated thousands of combinations of price performance of each of the stocks or other assets relative to one another. Now a $500 laptop can perform these calculations in seconds; that is one reason this type of analysis remains so popular in the professional investment community.

Let's look at a typical efficient frontier analysis, the kind we use in the investment advisory profession every day. Figure 12.2 shows

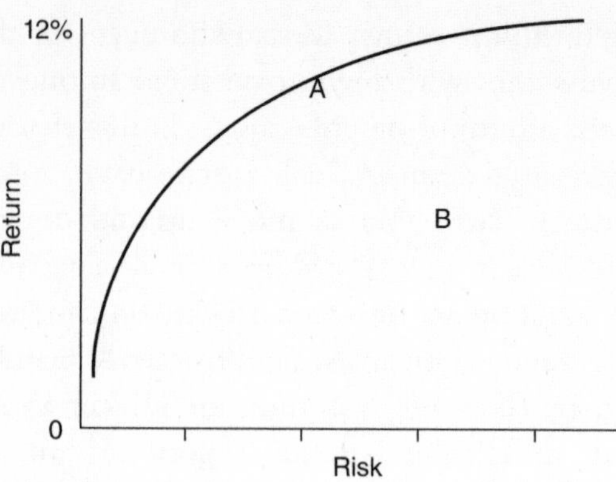

Figure 12.2 The Efficient Frontier
SOURCE: Lepercq Lynx Investment Advisory.

the analysis with the horizontal axis at the bottom representing risk as measured by standard deviation. You may recall that standard deviation is a measure of volatility as depicted in the Guassian bell curve (Figure 12.1). In investment terms, we consider a portfolio of investment assets riskier if its historic price range is very large and we consider one that has only moderate price movements less risky. The higher the standard deviation, the riskier the portfolio. Therefore, as you move to the right on the horizontal line, your risk is going up.

On the vertical axis you'll find your expected return, in this case from 0 percent to 12 percent measured annually. The curved line on the chart is Markowitz's efficient frontier, and here is the important message: *Your portfolio is efficient at any point on the line.* What that means is that at any point on the curve, your portfolio would have the highest expected return for a given amount of risk. Or, conversely, if you look at the risk axis, you can pick a level of risk and the efficient frontier would show an allocation that would provide the highest return for that level of assumed risk. What this also means that any portfolio on the curve would not benefit from additional diversification. Get on the curve, and you get it right!

Look at Portfolio A in Figure 12.2, which is on the curve with a return of 8 percent and a standard deviation of 14 percent. This investor has a portfolio that should produce the correct return for the risk he is willing to take. (Of course, time plays an important role in this discussion, and we will get to that shortly.) But what happens if after doing all the calculations, your portfolio is below the line, as is the case with Portfolio B? In that case, your portfolio is either too risky for the return you expect, or it is not getting enough return for the risk you are taking. In other words, your portfolio needs attention!

Now you can see why investment professionals love this exercise. You go to see them in their lovely offices, you bring your monthly brokerage statements with all of your holdings, and they will input the data and run an efficient frontier analysis for you. There is a very good chance that your existing portfolio will *not* be on the efficient frontier. You will be the holder of Portfolio B, or worse. Through the magic of modern finance, your prospective advisor will tell you that if you just hire them, they will be happy to create a much more efficient portfolio where the risks and rewards of your investment desires will be aligned.

James Tobin Enhances MPT

As good as Markowitz's concept of optimizing risk and return in a portfolio is, in the late 1950s another Nobel Prize winner, James Tobin, added some refinements and improvements to it. How can you improve the efficient frontier when building a portfolio? By adding risk-free assets to the mix. What are risk-free assets? These are bank deposits or U.S. Treasury securities. Since these are riskless investments, they have a standard deviation of zero, which is quite logical since standard deviation is a measure of volatility and risk.

Let's assume that Treasuries have a return of 5 percent. That's higher than the actual rate today but close to the historic rate of return. By adding risk-free assets to the risky assets in your efficient frontier portfolio, you can improve the risk and the return. In fact, the expected return will be the weighted return of the risk-free assets and the risky assets of the market portfolio.

Now look at Figure 12.3. Note that we have added a straight line that starts at the risk-free rate of 5 percent that we mentioned earlier and proceeds in a straight line to the point where it intercepts the efficient frontier. This line is known as the Capital Market Line, or

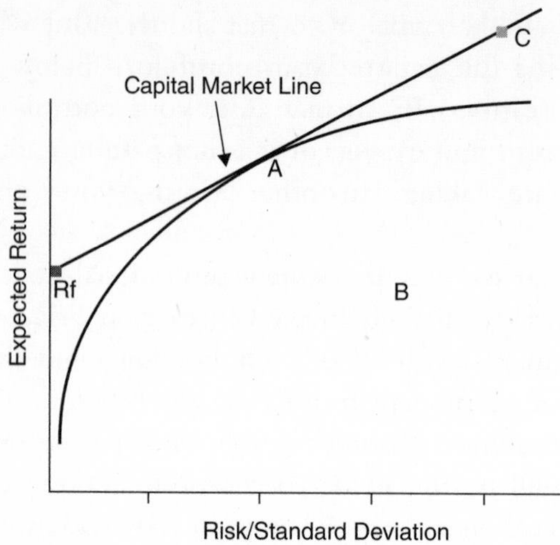

Figure 12.3 Efficient Frontier with Capital Market Line
SOURCE: Lepercq Lynx Investment Advisory.

CML. Tobin called the point where the CML intercepts the efficient frontier the super-efficient portfolio.

Here's why: An investor who holds a super-efficient portfolio has two additional investment options. He can sell the risk-free asset (Treasury bills) short; take in the cash, which costs him about 5 percent in interest; then invest the additional cash on the efficient frontier and earn about 10 percent for a net gain of an additional 5 percent over the cost of the amount he borrowed.

With the second option, a more conservative investor can sell some of the assets that are subject to market risk and invest these assets on the risk-free line, effectively buying Treasuries with no risk. So, he sells assets that have risk and substitutes assets with no risk. Both of these super-efficient portfolio strategies take the portfolio off of the efficient frontier and put them on the Capital Market Line in Figure 12.3.

What is truly interesting here is that any point on the Capital Market Line is more efficient (i.e., more return for the same risk or the same return for less risk) than the points on the efficient frontier. This is because the efficient frontier consists entirely of risky assets while the Capital Market Line adds risk-free assets to the mix.

Tobin advised that portfolio construction should be a two-step process. First, find the super-efficient portfolio. Then, if the investor can support more risk, leverage the portfolio by shorting the risk-free asset and buying more risky assets in the super-efficient portfolio. The second option is for a more conservative investor. In his case, that would involve deleveraging the super-efficient portfolio by selling some of the risky assets in the super-efficient portfolio and investing them in risk-free assets. As always, the objective is to achieve more return for the same risk or the same return for lower risk.

Time plays an important role in our discussion. As we know, in any given year, returns can cover a wide range. Investors on the efficient frontier count on the expected returns to be realized over a long time frame. Indeed, the investor who opts for a riskier portfolio with a higher expected return must not forget that he is assuming higher risk. That means that in any given year, results can fluctuate widely. This level of risk requires staying power and a strong stomach. Likewise, in the example we just discussed, using leverage to increase returns with Tobin's concept of the super-efficient portfolio may well subject the investor to some roller-coaster returns in the meantime.

To sum up, Modern Portfolio Theory, much in use today, attempts to quantify the risk you take when you invest. Put another way, what are the chances of achieving a decent return on my investment? Conversely, how much money could I lose with a portfolio that is configured like mine is? Harry Markowitz advanced our understanding of risk and taught us that we can reduce that risk substantially by diversifying our portfolio of securities intelligently. Informed investment professionals have been listening ever since.

A Matter of Time

Before we go on, let's discuss the role time plays in our understanding of risk and investment returns. You may be familiar with the term *reversion to the mean.* It's a fancy way to say that if a long-term average—in this case, the average investment return of the stock market over the last 90 years—is 9 percent a year, we know that this average return consists of annual returns that fluctuate widely. So if we experience a period during which the stock market goes up at a much higher rate than average, we can safely expect that this outperformance will be balanced at some time with a period of years when the stock market will perform below the average of 9 percent return. Think back to the 1990s. The stock market had returns of twice the 9 percent average for several years. Then in 2000, 2001, and 2002, the market suffered three years of losses. So in our discussion, "reversion to the mean" simply refers to the tendency of the market to go back to the historic average return over time. Periods of very high returns will be compensated for by periods of negative or very low returns. Indeed, that's what makes an average. The key phrase here is "over time," and we must cement its importance in our thinking about risk.

Here's why: A Wall Street maxim says that "time is your friend." Indeed. Investors who have been invested in stocks for decades enjoyed a return of about 9 percent a year. But what if you had just started investing a dozen years ago? Unfortunately, you would likely have lost money. As we pointed out in Chapter 9, from 1998 to 2008 the stock market return, as measured by the S&P 500, was *negative*. Yes, a loss, friends. And this example illustrates vividly why time is so important to investors. A university endowment arguably has an unlimited time objective. It lives on through many generations. That's one reason why university endowments don't invest like the rest of us. They can afford to tie up their money for many years in illiquid hedge funds and thousands of acres of timberland. They count on reversion to the mean if the stock market or some other asset class in which they are invested gets out of whack for a period of time.

Unfortunately, not all of us possess the luxury of unlimited time. A 75-year-old retiree can't afford to wait for his investments to revert to the mean because he may not be around when that happens. A 40 percent decline in the stock market, like we experienced in 2008, affects the retirement of millions of Americans who are in or approaching retirement. But over a 50-year time sequence of stock market returns, that 40 percent decline is barely a blip. Of course, in your retirement portfolio it is definitely not a blip, but a serious loss that will be hard to make up in a few years or even a decade. So keep in mind throughout our discussion of risk that both time and covariance play a very important role in the expected outcomes of our investments.

A Fly in the Ointment, Part I

First, let's talk about what's good about Modern Portfolio Theory before we discuss a fly in the ointment

Markowitz's contribution to our understanding of risk in the stock market cannot be overestimated. For generations, investment professionals, typically bankers in three-piece suits working out of wood-paneled trust company offices, evaluated the risk of each security one by one. "Let's see, these steel and railroad stocks are safe and pay good dividends, so we'll load the portfolios up with these safe selections." We know now that this practice ignores the covariance of these stocks, or the fact that these stocks tend to behave in similar stock market patterns, so that old practice of loading up on "safe" stocks will not effectively diversify your portfolio.

What good old Harry taught us through his elegant set of mathematics of diversification is that risk is determined not by simply adding up the risk of each stock in your portfolio, but rather by the risk of the portfolio as a whole. Indeed, in some cases, adding a risky asset class, like emerging market stocks, might actually *reduce* the volatility, or riskiness, of the portfolio as a whole. So Markowitz's contribution to investment theory is enormous.

Similarly, Friederich Gauss's contributions to mathematics and investment theory are numerous and enduring. The bell curve, which he popularized, helped us understand the concept of diversification through the analysis of uncorrelated asset classes. In pointing out some of the problems that have emerged with tools such as the efficient frontier and the bell curve in analyzing the risks in investing, we do not intend to repudiate the extraordinary contributions made by Gauss, Markowitz, and others to our understanding of portfolio creation and risk management.

This short history of investment theory leads us to the present day, and to the recent crisis. In 2008, the stock market lost almost 40 percent in a single year, a record loss that had been unmatched in severity since the Great Depression. Then, in early 2009, it got worse before it turned around. The sickening and seemingly endless decline led many investors and academics to ask serious questions about our understanding of risk. Indeed, what use are all of the discoveries made in investment theory if, despite the great theories and Nobel Prize accolades, we can still lose almost half of our wealth in a breathtaking 18 months? The magnitude of the losses incurred from late 2007 to early 2009 might well take a generation to recover! Many investors do not have that luxury of time. In the worst of cases, retirees who went though that trauma abandoned retirement and started looking for jobs or drastically scaled down their standards of living. So the question of the moment is: Can we avoid this type of personal financial disaster in the future?

We believe we can. First, meet Benoit Mandelbrot.

Who Is Benoit Mandelbrot and Why Is Everyone Talking about Him?

Benoit Mandelbrot was a French mathematician. He was born in Warsaw and his family moved to France from Poland in 1936 after they predicted the coming threat to Jewish families posed by the rising Nazi Party in Germany. Mandelbrot studied in France and was admitted to the prestigious École Polytechnique in the late 1940s. He subsequently studied at the California Institute of Technology, went back to France and earned a PhD in mathematics at the University of Paris. In 1958, he and his wife moved to the United States, where Mandelbrot joined the research staff at IBM, where he remained for 30 years. He subsequently joined the faculty at Yale as a professor in mathematics. He died on October 14, 2010, at the age of 85.[4]

Mandelbrot was a superb mathematician, to be sure, but his theories are of special interest to the financial community. Indeed, Mandelbrot fundamentally changed how we look at risk in the stock market. He is the father of fractal geometry. This is admittedly a complicated form of math in both practice and theory, so we'll try to boil it down to the fundamentals of what this branch of math does. Then we'll explain why it has become so important to the analysis of risk in the stock market.

When we study shapes, forms, and patterns, we look for symmetry. Geometry is a good example with its squares, rectangles, triangles, and other forms that no matter their size, follow uniform patterns of construction. The fractal view of the world assumes that patterns of phenomena or even objects in the world are not stable; that is, they do not follow a neat order structure or pattern. What is interesting about all this to us investors is that when we look at risk using the Gaussian bell curve, we are, in fact, showing probability along a neat distribution where the most frequent occurrences are found at the center of the bell curve and the rarer events, the outliers, fall neatly at the extremes to the right and left.

Mandelbrot saw the world differently. Have a look at the coast of England from a satellite; it appears very orderly and linear. But as you get closer, you notice the cliffs and rocks, the shifting coastlines and beaches, and all kinds of craggy land following no pattern at all. Another example: When you see a tree, you instantly know it's a tree even though you have never seen this particular tree before. In fact, this tree looks like most other trees of the same variety. Yet its leaves have a particular pattern, as do its branches, which are formed as a little tree with branches off its main stem, and of course the tree itself has a trunk with branches that shoot off its base form. And they are all different.

You may well conclude that these observations are hardly mind bending. That trees and coastlines follow irregular shapes is not a difficult concept to grasp. Indeed, our own observations readily confirm these facts. The problem is that this irregular and unpredictable pattern of phenomena is important to understand in the context of our estimates of future events, and in our case, what might happen to the stock market.

Look at the bell curve in Figure 12.4. This time, we have added the standard deviation lines on this neatly shaped bell curve. You can see that the curve doesn't accommodate much more than three standard deviations. A three standard deviation event is rare indeed, 1 in 100.

The main debate sparked by Mandelbrot is that market crashes and other investment phenomena that may cost us our life savings are far more likely occurrences than existing investment theories have suggested. This is the fly in the Modern Portfolio Theory ointment

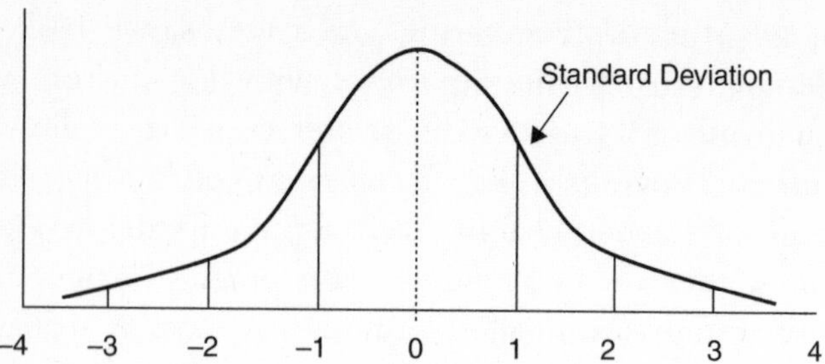

Figure 12.4 Bell Curve with Standard Deviation
SOURCE: Lepercq Lynx Investment Advisory.

and it is indeed earthshaking. Nassim Nicholas Taleb, a brilliant mathematical investor/philosopher, wrote a hugely popular best-selling book, *The Black Swan* (Random House, 2007), a book dedicated to Benoit Mandelbrot. In his provocative and lively book, Taleb points out that what we don't know is far more relevant to our lives and fortunes than what we do know or think we know. It is about the unexpected nature of randomness. (In fact, Taleb's earlier book, also a best-seller, was *Fooled by Randomness*.)

The title of his book, *The Black Swan,* refers to the fact that for centuries, most of the world assumed that all swans were white. Indeed, no one had ever seen a black swan, so it was a pretty safe bet that all swans are white. And that was true until travel to Australia became more popular and the rest of the world discovered its population of black swans. Taleb dubbed a "Black Swan event" (capitalized) as an incident that is vastly more severe than that of the discovery of the black bird. Its main characteristic is that it carries large consequences when it occurs, while being incomputable mathematically. Mandelbrot refutes the bell curve, establishing that Gauss's distribution does not track outliers, and proposes his method to calculate the probability of these events. Taleb goes beyond Mandelbrot and refuses all computability for this class of events, establishing that Black Swans are beyond the domain of mathematics. Where Taleb and Mandelbrot agree is that using the fractal framework, some swans can turn gray, but not all, and not all the time.

In that, Taleb falls squarely in the skeptical tradition, with a class of philosophers such as David Hume and Karl Popper. But his idea is to suspend skepticism outside the areas in which Black Swans can be harmful, and establish the limits of such a domain, which he calls the "fourth quadrant." In it, Taleb's proposal is to switch from attempts to calculate the risks of these events to identifying fragilities and vulnerabilities—and debt is what causes the most fragility in the financial system.[5]

The result is that the neat distribution of probability and risk in Modern Portfolio Theory needs at best an asterisk and at worst a fire alarm bell to explain that risk is sometimes not as neat and symmetrical as the graph represented. This caveat notwithstanding, Markowitz's theory still has appeal and value. With it, the investment return outlook for your entire portfolio depends on two numbers based on reward and risk, or in statistical terms, mean and variance along with the covariance of the different asset classes your portfolio may hold. With this construct, you can estimate the return you might get over time from your portfolio along with the statistical odds of actually getting your expected return. That's pretty neat. How do you do this? You estimate the growth of your stock portfolio using, perhaps, the long-term return on stocks over many decades. Then you analyze the volatility of your portfolio by looking at how much each of the groups of holdings fluctuated over the past years. For example, if you own small cap stocks and this asset class moved up or down by an average of 15 percent a year over the past 10 years, you will assume that that trend in volatility is likely to continue. So we calculate the range of returns of all the asset classes in your portfolio over the next five years on the bell curve (Figure 12.4). The calculations, done by computer, incorporate thousands of different combinations of possibilities, worst-case to best-case, over a five-year period. When the probabilities are all calculated, the curve will show you that this portfolio has a 90 percent chance of having an annual return for the next five years ranging from 2 percent per annum to 14 percent per annum while the most likely return, the 50 percent line at the fattest part of the curve, shows an annualized return over five years of 8 percent.

Of course, as we discussed earlier, the longer the time span, the more likely the chances that your average return will be achieved (Figure 12.5). The range of annual returns shrinks over the years.

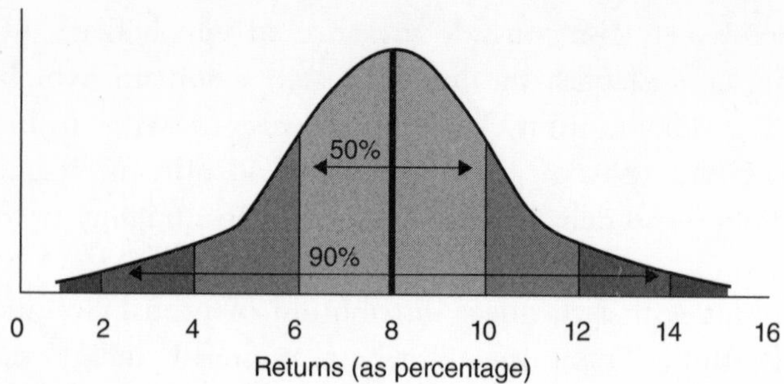

Figure 12.5 Bell Curve with Returns
SOURCE: Lepercq Lynx Investment Advisory.

Remember the discussion of the 1-year loss of 40 percent, as happened in 2008? Over a 50-year period, that 40 percent 1-year decline would barely move the needle on the long-term return of 8 percent. But for how many decades can you live with a 40 percent decline in the value of your stocks in a single year?

The Fly in the Ointment, Part II

Another problem with the Gaussian bell curve is that it does not accurately reflect the "tail risk." So let's talk about tail risk. Notice how the tails of the curve slope down from the mean in a beautifully symmetric shape. The point made by Mandelbrot, Taleb, and others who follow fractal geometry is that the perfectly symmetrical shape of the curve is an illusion. In the real world, the roughness of the curve, and the roughness of life, means that unpredictable events will occur and by definition they will be events we cannot anticipate. And here is the key point: *These events will occur far more frequently than the bell curve analysis suggests, and the events will be far larger and more damaging.* In other words, the tails are generally fatter than the bell curve suggests. Look again at a bell curve, this time in Figure 12.6.

Augustin Louis Cauchy: He Knew about Fat Tails!

Another great French mathematician, Augustin Louis Cauchy (1789–1857), may well have understood probability better than did Harry

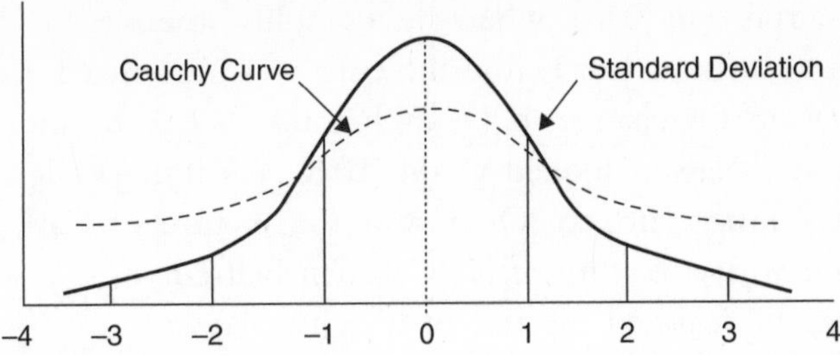

Figure 12.6 Bell Curve with Cauchy Fat Tails
SOURCE: Lepercq Lynx Investment Advisory.

Markowitz or any of Markowitz's predecessors. (Indeed, the French are not only good at making wine and champagne, but they also have excelled in math!) Cauchy launched the theory of functions of a complex variable, and don't worry if you don't know what that means. The mathematicians will know. More important to us is what Cauchy had to say about probability and its application to standard deviation.

In Figure 12.6, we indicated with a dotted line a curve technically known as a Cauchy curve along with the Gaussian bell curve, which you are already familiar with. Although the curves look similar, the difference between Cauchy and Gaussian is fundamental. Note that the Gaussian curve falls off rapidly as it gets away from the central region, whereas the Cauchy curve has fat, extended "tails." (For the technical crowd: The curve is also known as a special case of 'student's t distribution' with a degree of freedom of one.) Because the decrease to infinity is slow, the Cauchy distribution has no mean and therefore no standard deviation, and it is outside the realm of Central Limit Theorem. The importance of this to our discussion is that the Cauchy curve clearly indicates that the tail, or rare events, are more likely than suggested by the Gaussian bell curve. If only we had paid more attention to Cauchy a few years ago!

Imagine then, that the Gaussian bell curve, a pillar of Modern Portfolio Theory, may be very, very wrong in estimating our risk in the stock market. Oh, Freddie Gauss, have you misled us? No one is more upset with him than *The Black Swan* author, Nassim Nicholas Taleb, who recounts in his book a story of his travels through the

Frankfurt airport in 2001 when he used his stopover to buy dark chocolates. In this era just before the euro was introduced, the cashier handed Nassim his change in Deutschmarks. While he munched on the chocolate, Nassim looked at the 10 Deutschmark bill he got in change and nearly choked. On it was the picture of Carl Friedrich Gauss along with a picture of his Gaussian bell curve![6] Nassim didn't say whether he finished the rest of his chocolates.

Let's look at some specific examples of rare events and their odds, according to the bell curve. In his book, *The (Mis)behavior of Markets,* Mandelbrot cites a 2002 Citigroup study on currency price swings. On one day, the dollar rose against the Japanese yen by 3.78 percent, which is five standard deviations from the average. On the Gaussian bell curve, this would happen only once in a century. In the same study, the biggest currency decline of the yen versus the dollar was 7.9 percent. The odds of that happening, based on the bell curve and standard deviation: once in every 15 billion years![7]

Here is another example to ponder. In August 1998, a number of unpleasant occurrences caused a near panic in the stock and currency markets. The U.S. president was fighting an impeachment by Congress, the Chinese were rumored to be considering a devaluation of their currency, and Russia was enduring a cash squeeze and nearing default on its bonds. The combination of these problems caused rising discomfort on Wall Street, and the stock market reacted predictably and swiftly. On August 4, 1998, the Dow Jones Average declined 3.5 percent. The crushing blow came on August 31, when the market tumbled a dizzying 6.8 percent, a veritable meltdown.

Back to Modern Portfolio Theory probability. What are the chances of a one-day decline in the U.S. stock market of 6.8 percent? One in 20 million. If you were a daily stock trader you would not expect to see such an occurrence in 100,000 years of trading. And the odds of getting three daily declines of over 3.5 percent in a single month, which happened in August 1998, is about one in 500 *billion*.

Rare indeed. Or was it? Mandelbrot points out that in 1997, the Dow had fallen 7.7 percent in a single day. The odds of that happening are one in 50 billion. And, of course, there was the crash of October 19, 1987, when the market tumbled an almost incredible

29 percent. The odds of that happening are virtually incalculable. A number for that probability would not have any meaning.

How about another recent example? On October 15, 2008, the Dow tumbled by 7.87 percent. The probability of that happening, using the bell curve analysis, is one in 50 billion. So after that traumatic day, you were safe for another 50 billion years, right? Maybe not. Just 45 days later, on December 1, 2008, the market, as measured by the Dow, again fell 7.7 percent.

Let's look back at the history of the stock market and see if the bell curve probability stood the test of time. We mentioned earlier in this section that according to the Gaussian bell curve, the odds of three daily stock market declines of 3.5 percent or more in a single month are about one in 500 billion (yes, *billion*). If that's true, we would be lucky, or unlucky, to encounter such a month once in a lifetime. Well, let's look back at the Dow Jones Average, which has a record back to 1928. Now let's count the number of times there was a daily decline of 3.5 percent or more in a single month. How many would you guess? One, maybe two? We counted 26 months in which there were three or more daily declines of 3.5 percent or more in a month since 1928! Does a single occurrence like that sound like a one in 500 million probability?

One final example: We cited earlier that the bell curve chances of a one-day decline in the U.S. stock market of 6.8 percent were one in 20 million. A daily stock trader would not expect to see such an occurrence if he traded for 100,000 years. Here's the reality check: Since 1928, there have been 25 instances of the Dow Jones average losing 6.80 percent or more in a single day.

Are You Getting the Picture Now?

Let's see: If a one in 50 billion chance event happens, then a similar event happens again fairly soon thereafter, and if we have a succession of these highly improbable events happening at regular intervals, what might you conclude? We can think of only one answer: *The odds are wrong!* Mandelbrot's (and Taleb's) point is that the Gaussian bell curve and its neatly defined probability statistics do not represent the reality of how often tumultuous and tragic events really do occur. Mandelbrot's fractal geometry tells us that the world is not a smooth, orderly place. Reality is tinged with roughness. Here's a simple example: When a child draws a mountain, a cloud, or a Christmas tree, what does it look like? We easily imagine the straight lines and smooth curves of these drawings. But we also know that this is not what they really look like! In Mandelbrot's own words:

> *Clouds are not spheres, mountains are not cones, coastlines are not circles, and bark is not smooth, nor does lightning travel in a straight line.*[8]

Risk is also not symmetrical, the bell curve is not accurate about risk, and catastrophic events like market crashes occur far more often than the investment community has assumed based on the theories that have guided the industry for a long time. And remember, risk does not always result in tragedy. Risk is sometimes rewarded. Indeed, in 2009, the stock market had a violent and swift recovery from its lows in March, rising over 50 percent by the end of summer.

In short, we thought we understood risk, but we didn't.

Here's why this is important. We must reassess stock market risk and put aside the old theories. Remember: We are willing to incur risk because we want to capture reward. With reward comes the risk that we won't get it. We invest in a portfolio of stocks because we expect our investments to grow over the years and increase our fortunes. Most of the time, for prudent and savvy investors, that will happen. For others it won't, and the losses may well be catastrophic. With a new and deeper understanding of the risks in investing, we firmly believe that the chances that your portfolio will achieve your expected return are significantly enhanced. This is particularly important in the perilous times we face. A financial meltdown will highlight the risks we all face in investing. That's why it is so important to understand financial risk.

The major lesson of the past is that we must be prepared for cataclysmic market declines that will occur more than once every few billion years. With a new and fresh understanding of stock market risk, especially in the poisonous financial environment that lies ahead, we can begin to construct a more intelligent portfolio that will see us through the crisis.

To be clear, Mandelbrot's contribution to our understanding of risk is highly important in that it debunks the neat and symmetric distributions and probability of the bell curve when it comes to the frequency of calamitous financial market events. What Mandelbrot's work *does not do* is tell us when or how frequently these catastrophic events will occur. It does not provide someone along the way who will wave a red flag and say: "Watch out! Danger ahead!" Instead, his work cautions us not to rely on the old theories of probability.

Conclusion

Modern Portfolio Theory, with its bell curve and asset allocation, has many useful features. Markowitz's contribution to our knowledge of investing is firmly implanted and will remain an important addition to investment theory and practice. But the part of the theory that involves the bell curve is *wrong*. We must not be lulled into a false sense of security through the probability estimates of the standard bell curve. If we have learned anything from the recent market collapse it is this: Turbulent, even catastrophic, markets will occur *far more frequently* than we originally thought. Similarly, positive market surprises will also occur. Risk works both ways. The challenge is to understand the dangers that lurk before us and to recognize what they mean and how we might protect our assets and our wealth. There is little we can do to prevent the coming demise of the world's financial system, but there are many things we can do to ensure that our personal wealth does not follow the crisis down a road to ruinous losses.

Conclusion

We Have Been Here Before

This is hardly the first time the global economy has been held in the death-like grip of debts and deficits, spurred by profligate spending, poor policy decisions, and Black Swan–type events. Countries have defaulted on debts, interest rates have soared, and consumers have seen their savings disappear and paychecks turned to nearly worthless paper as the escalating costs of goods and services eroded the value of their hard-earned money.

Yes, we have been here before.

Sovereign governments have refused to rein in massive public entitlement giveaways. Government capital projects have spun wildly out of control, thanks to patronage and lack of oversight. States and localities have dug themselves huge trenches into which they've carelessly tossed piles of their constituents' money. Global dominoes have crashed into one another, making one nation's economic sickness an entire world's fiscal flu pandemic.

For sure, we have been here before.

Policy makers have recklessly cranked up the printing presses and devalued their currencies with the mistaken belief that it would generate lasting wealth. Deficits have run amok in the interest of financing national war machines, without any thought to how such damage will be undone when the bills come due. Fiscally irresponsible global governments have found themselves suddenly ostracized by their trading partners and forced to jack up the interest paid on their debt in the hopes that some generous soul might buy it to keep the wheels turning.

Indeed, we have been here before.

Three millennia of fiscal and monetary mistakes are easily researchable to show us that this is not the first time the world has found itself plunging down the debt-and-deficit Rabbit Hole. In this book, we've traced a very long path from the days of ancient Rome through the Weimar Republic, Hungary, Zimbabwe, and the United States in the 1970s to the present day, where our biggest crisis has germinated and is ready to spread throughout the global economy. Like Alice's journey behind the white rabbit and through the realm of Wonderland, our next stop is the Pool of Tears.

So if we've had such a long history of these types of problems, how did we get here again? Well, it's not like we weren't warned.

While politicians, policy makers, and TV-ready economists were banging the deflation drum throughout 2009 and 2010 as justification for artificially low interest rates, debt-feeding stimulus programs, and dollar debasing, others were quietly warning that inflation would be the economy's greatest enemy. After all, there was certainly plenty of ammunition if one could just look beyond government statistics that long ago ceased to be meaningful when measuring true inflationary threats.

One of the most compelling warnings we came across in researching this book was a little-noticed eight-page analysis from the nonpartisan Congressional Budget Office released on July 27, 2010.[1] The study accurately diagnoses the looming financial crisis without resorting to hysterics. Hyperbole is unnecessary, in fact, when looking at the factors just in the American economy alone that will create an inflationary if not hyperinflationary environment. The problems in the United States are but one factor in what will generate a global financial meltdown that will make what happened in 2008 and 2009 seem like nothing more than the proverbial canary in the coal mine.

"A Sudden Financial Crisis"

The United States has long held more debt than advisable, but the problem has become far more pernicious in the past three years. We are nearing a point where our debt will equal and then exceed our total gross domestic product. Though we are fed a steady diet of persuasion that the debt and deficits we've acquired since the onset of the financial crisis were necessary to right our leaking ship, there seems to be little care as to how and when we get ourselves out of this mess. By 2015 the total debt service could exceed $1 trillion.[2] For those of us who believe that the country is borrowing too much money and is headed toward a devastating day of reckoning, this is an alarming figure.

We are not alone.

Warnings abound for the emerging crisis. The CBO also cautioned a year ago that the United States faces the danger of "a sudden financial crisis" for which the date is "unknown, in part because the ratio of federal debt to GDP is climbing into unfamiliar territory and in part because the risk of a crisis is influenced by a number of other factors, including the government's long-term budget outlook, its near-term borrowing needs, and the health of the economy. When fiscal crises do occur, they often happen during an economic downturn, which amplifies the difficulties of adjusting fiscal policy in response."[3] When the crisis comes, the CBO warns, remedies will be "limited and unattractive."[4]

To address a few of the CBO's concerns, we first can safely and uncompromisingly say that the U.S. government's "long-term budget outlook" is bleak. Entitlement programs remain sacrosanct in large part because chipping away at the government's social safety net is hugely unpopular and always subject to backlash, no matter how much public opinion surveys may find that most Americans favor austerity. One need look no further than the 2010 riots across the European Union nations, where folks of every stripe took to the streets to protest measures ranging from raising the retirement age to increasing college tuition.

A question we hear recurrently is, "Do you think that could happen here?" The short answer is that of course it could happen here. While the virulence of such protests would be hard to gauge, frustrated Americans tired of welfare for Wall Street and ineffectual stimulus programs carried out while unemployment persists at perilously high levels cannot be expected to act in a civil manner when they see grand-scale cuts. So it's easy to assume that budgetary constraints are unlikely to abate until sustained, significant growth is achieved and a more responsible fiscal air permeates Washington.

Secondly, governmental "near-term borrowing needs" remain substantial. This is true not only in the United States but also throughout the developed world. An expected slow global economic recovery will depress tax revenues in nations where large percentages of budgets are composed of fixed costs. In the United States, the situation is compounded by the government's need to continue borrowing to feed various stimulus programs and to finance its budget deficit of more than $1 trillion. The International Monetary Fund has called this need for short-term borrowing in sovereign debt "the newest threat to the financial system." And the Government Accountability Office (GAO) said late in 2010 that even in the most optimistic scenario, in which the ObamaCare plan actually reduces health care costs and other economic conditions improve, "it is clear over the long term, historical levels of spending and revenue cannot be maintained going forward."[5] Suffice it to say then that the government's near-term borrowing needs meet the CBO's second criterion for a fiscal crisis to take place.

Finally, let's look at the health of the economy, cited by the CBO as its third contingency when examining what danger the future holds. This, indeed, is the great wild card. As 2011 progressed, unemployment was improving but still dire, the housing market remained a mess, and other aspects, such as manufacturing and various demand gauges, presented a mixed bag. But while the economy tries to grow organically, it faces numerous headwinds, none more than the debts and deficits that always, always retard economic growth. The reason for this in part is that every dollar used by the public sector is a dollar not used by the private sector.

If you believe that the government does a better job spending money than private industry and normal taxpayers like us, then you're not troubled by this trend. But if you maintain that capital is better used by private industry, whether it's construction, finance, or Harry the Barber down at the corner, then it's hard to understand how directing what will be more than 20 percent of our entire budget toward paying down debt is a good thing.

This is what economists call "opportunity cost." While spending nearly a trillion dollars bailing out the banking system may be looked back on as a necessary evil, it's hard not to wonder what that money might have done had it been placed in other hands. (Let it be stated here: We have no great qualms with the Troubled Asset Relief Program, commonly known as TARP, nor any of its alphabet-soup brethren. Instead, we rue the conditions that brought us to the point where such extreme, unprecedented measures had to be taken and wonder whether anyone is understanding that the climate of debt that permeates our economic culture ultimately is what created the financial crisis.) Opportunity cost, in any of its forms, is a terrible thing, and the most ponderous element of the financial crisis going forward is what we lost in having to backtrack and fix all that went wrong.

And so that delivers us to this point in the book, where we bring all the elements leading to the next phase of the crisis together under one literary roof. In trying to escape a crisis brought on by debts and deficits, we as a global society have prescribed . . . debt and deficits. Indeed, the path to the crash ahead is not a loop-de-loop or even a road traveled by that meandering country mile. Instead, our looming financial crisis has weathered a fairly straight course.

Walking the Line

In delineating our path we have followed a specific school of thought—epistemic humility. That's a fancy-sounding term but one that has simplicity at its core. It is the pursuit of knowledge without using leaps of faith, or lack thereof. It is drawing conclusions based not on intuition or what we think might happen somewhere down the road. It is a thought pattern free of confirmation bias—in other words, looking only at evidence that supports our thesis. We believe we cannot predict what will happen in the markets tomorrow, but by using linear thinking we find that the global economy is heading for a massive collapse because of inflation, which itself will be driven by defaults and by soaring interest rates to finance the world's debts.

Epistemic humility is the opposite, in fact the enemy of, epistemic arrogance. The former seeks not to divine from tea leaves or intuition or some short-term chart pattern what might happen in the next 10 minutes. Instead, it seeks to use prevailing, demonstrable, irrefutable conditions to show what will happen over a course of time. Epistemic arrogance comes from groupthink that refuses to account for what *Black Swan* author Nassim Nicholas Taleb refers to as "the highly improbable consequential event" that misses detection because of "the scandal of prediction."[6] This blissful ignorance was seen at every turn as we were writing this book, from talking heads on television who insisted there is too much "slack" in the economy for inflation to occur, all the way up to academicians, economists, and policy makers who reasoned that because traditional metrics were failing to show inflation in a traditional way, then it simply could not exist. There were no black swans either, of that we were sure, until evidence came along to show that there are. Not having evidence to prove something is not quite the same as having evidence to disprove it. And there *is* evidence to show that inflation is barreling straight at us. But, strangely, policy makers continue to behave as if inflation is our friend, as if once the monster gets up off the table Dr. Frankenstein will be able to keep him from massacring an entire global economic system.

The path this monster follows is relatively easy to trace.

It starts somewhere in Europe, where troubled economies no longer can pay their bills and one fairly good-sized country—say, Spain or Greece or Portugal—has to go through what is politely called a "restructuring." This is an Orwellian economic synonym for "default," and it will have repercussions across the continent, then across the globe.

How do we know one of these countries will default? Because there simply is no other way. Countries in the nations we refer to as the PIIGS—Portugal, Ireland, Italy, Greece, and Spain—have reached points where the imploding economies and suffocating debt are making it impossible for them to meet their financial obligations. While the International Monetary Fund, of which the United States is the largest contributor, stands at the ready with a massive bailout fund, the interconnected nature of the European Union makes a financial crisis a certainty.

Remember, this is not a prediction. We attach no specific date to which our extrasensory perception mechanisms indicate. The discipline of epistemic humility leads us to say only that such a crisis is a certainty and the only unknowns here are when and how much. We know that when countries reach the level of debt-to-GDP of the PIIGS nations, default, or restructuring, is the only possible outcome for those nations to meet their obligations. We also know that when nations must restructure their debts, two things happen. The first is that those holding the debt will be forced to take what is known as a "haircut," or a severe discount on the value of the bonds. Where investors who bought the original notes might expect to receive a dollar for a dollar, plus whatever coupon and yield the notes held, they now will have to accept new obligations that are worth perhaps 30 percent or even less of the original purchase price. On top of that, the money will not be paid back under the same terms, so a debt that once had a 5-year maturity now will have a 7- or 10-year maturity or worse.

The second thing that will happen is that whoever buys this debt as part of the restructuring will demand a higher return for the investment. That means issuing mid- to long-term debt at 5 or 6 percent interest now will require double or triple the yield. Imagine what this will do to the coffers of countries that are already strapped for cash. Then imagine what it will mean to the creditors of these nations, knowing that they have lost billions of dollars on what was supposed to be a sure thing: the debt of a nation backed up by the full faith and credit that had suddenly become almost worthless.

The global financial community, despite spanning continents, time zones, and oceans, is a small world. Countries and their financial institutions keep a close scorecard on how nations handle their debts, including the policies they enact on both a fiscal and monetary basis. Those who default face punishment and are ostracized. It happened with Argentina in 2002, it will happen with Greece or whichever of the PIIGS is to default first, and it will happen to the United States when the nation finds itself in a colossal bind when debt passes GDP, an ignominious event that could happen as soon as 2011. The day of reckoning may not immediately fall upon the United States, but it looms.

How this episode plays out is yet to be seen, and we will not predict its date lest we display epistemic arrogance. However, we do know that the current cost of servicing the national debt is 10 percent of total revenue and trending well higher as the country continues an inexorable march toward debt hell, the depths of which the government cannot even comprehend at this point. The CBO has stated the debt-to-GDP ratio will hit 90 percent by 2020; a Treasury department report last year pegged the figure at 102 percent by 2015, the same year the national debt is likely to hit $19.6 trillion!

When a nation's debt service hits 18 percent of its budget, the rating agencies put that country on their credit "watch" lists, an ominous signal that a downgrade could be on the horizon. While the United States has never been the recipient of a downgrade, a plethora of saber-rattling over the past three years leads to the conclusion that such a move is not out of the question. As unique a set of circumstances that a downgrade would bring, it would be met by an equally forceful response that would set the stage for the worst part of the global financial crisis.

Faced with the inability to pay off its debts, the United States would never default. Instead, the nation would accelerate an action that many monetary policy critics believe is already well in effect but with a name that policy makers dare not speak, namely to monetize the debt. What that means in simple terms is that the Federal Reserve itself would pay the government's debts by printing money. We have discussed at length what happens when the supply of money increases dramatically, as it has over the past three years. Sooner or later all that supply will exact a price.

Dallas Federal Reserve President Richard Fisher gave a speech on November 8, 2010, that should be required hearing not only for his colleagues but also for all policy makers and for that matter anyone who thinks we're not on a slippery slope of monetization. Here is a bit of the speech:

> *We know that once a central bank is perceived as targeting government debt yields at a time of persistent budget deficits, concern about debt monetization quickly arises. . . . Here we suffer from fiscal incontinence and regulatory misfeasance. If this were to change, I might advocate for accommodation.*

> *But that is not yet happening. And I worry that by providing monetary accommodation, we are reducing the odds that fiscal discipline will be brought to bear.*[7]

Such warnings went unheeded even though internal dissension at the Fed grew. At the time, the point of no return for the United States and its debt-deficit-inflation spiral was only beginning. Inflation doves believe that should debt monetization begin to cause runaway inflation, the Fed can step in and use fiscal tightening to reverse the effects. But what escapes this oversimplified worldview is that because the problems are global, not merely domestic, the central bank may well be powerless to halt this maddening whirlwind once it hits hurricane stage. That's because another brewing storm will go beyond debts and deficits, and it is one that neither Ben Bernanke nor anyone else in Washington will be able to stop.

Inflation from Abroad

Debts and deficits create their own inflation as a nation's economic standing comes into question and it must pay higher and higher prices to sell its debt. That in turn generates higher interest rates, which in a positive sense help pay down the debt more easily but in a negative sense drive the costs of everything else higher. Whether it's paying for a gallon of gas or checking out at the supermarket, the cycle exacts a cost at every level of society.

Indeed, when the United States cheapens its currency there are many, many repercussions. On Wall Street, a cheaper U.S. dollar helped exports and made stocks seem far less expensive, driving up the equity markets, and sending the major indices to a stunning rally off the March 2009 lows. But all of this dollar debasement came with a price. Commodity prices had become depressed in the wake of the banking and real estate crisis, dipping so dramatically that consumers were able to buy gas briefly for less than $2 a gallon and the cost of consumer goods almost across the board became at least marginally more affordable. But when the Fed set sail for its multiple rounds of quantitative easing, it took commodity prices with it.

A cheaper greenback greatly helps commodities like oil, gold, and grains, which are priced in U.S. dollars. Those same commodities can be purchased much more inexpensively with appreciating foreign currencies, sending their nominal values skyrocketing as 2011 began.

In the latter part of 2010 alone, cotton prices soared nearly 80 percent from August to November, while corn, used ubiquitously in the making of other products as well as by itself, jumped 55 percent from July to November. As a result, price inflation began creeping into the economy. Even as the government and its select bag of goods that go into the Consumer Price Index showed only incremental gains, consumers knew better. Gasoline and grocery bills jumped. The Standard & Poor's GSCI agricultural commodities index posted a gain of about 15 percent in 2010 and another 7 percent in the first two months of 2011, while the corresponding precious metals index soared nearly 30 percent. The notion that these costs won't be passed onto consumers is laughable. Ephraim Leibtag, senior economist for the Department of Agriculture's Economic Research Service, said in a CNBC.com article (written by coauthor of this book Cox) that price inflation certainly would pick up over the next six to nine months.[8]

Importantly, it is not just monetary policy to blame, so consequently it is far from monetary policy alone that will control this phenomenon as it accelerates. Commodity inflation is being driven strongly by demand from developing countries that need more food, metals, and other supplies to nourish their growing economies. The demand for copper, considered one of the most reliable economic gauges due to its need in construction, is expected to jump 15 percent in both China and India, and its price movements are sure to reflect that trend. China makes up fully 35 percent of global copper demand, so even if other economies shrink it will matter little to the metal's price (understanding that all asset prices, and particularly commodities, undergo gyrations and won't make a straight line higher).

The bottom line is that even if the Fed does react aggressively with monetary policy and finds some success when confronted with inflation, the central bank's effectiveness will be muted due to factors beyond its control. Debt and deficits will be the hammer, while commodity demand will be the nail that drives inflation in the United States and throughout the developed and developing world.

What can be done?

Putting the Genie Back in the Bottle

Herein we prescribe a comprehensive list of solutions to a problem that escapes easy remedies. If you're a policy maker, the short answer is to veer from the current path immediately and begin preparing to undo the programs that, while perhaps necessary at the time, will envelop the economy if not wound down in an expedient but not reckless manner. If you're an investor, you have several options, from precious metals to the class of bonds that guard against inflation to the stocks of solid dividend-paying companies that can withstand an inflationary environment. While the choices can be summed up broadly in one paragraph, they will require deft portfolio management that takes into account what are sure to be highly volatile times.

We've taken great pains throughout this book to avoid politics even while criticizing many of the decisions made by politicians. Trying to pin this crisis on one political party, one ideology, or one particular decision is a fool's game. The mistakes, like during so many other crises before it, run through both sides of the aisle, their origins based sometimes on noble goals—extending home ownership, to name one—and sometimes not so noble—cooking up ways to funnel money to pet legislative projects, to name one on the other side of the spectrum. The most important point is that this is a bipartisan problem that, while created by politicians, must be solved without politics to the greatest degree possible. In polarized times such as we've seen in the United States and around the world, such an aspiration may seem foolhardy. Perhaps from it inspiration will be born.

So let's start with policy, on the monetary side, to be specific. The monetization of the nation's debt will not have a happy ending, but the progressive unwinding of our current position will help cushion the blow. Remember, when Ronald Reagan tapped Paul Volcker and Arthur Laffer to chart his economic course, things looked pretty desperate as well. For a while, things got worse. Eventually they turned, leaving in their wake still more challenges but yet an opportunity to build on what had been accomplished during that decade. In the 1990s, faced with more fiscal problems, the Clinton administration and Congress forged a tenuous peace that allowed for what now seem like a few glorious, fleeting moments of a balanced budget and at least the promise of fiscal stability. Of course, the dot-com bust and the era of easy money were not far behind, followed by the unspeakable tragedy of 9/11, and once again we found ourselves trying to dig out of a hole.

On the political side, the challenges will be no less onerous. The Republican victory in the November 2010 elections was far more a repudiation of the politics-as-usual crowd that had overrun Washington than it was any mandate for the Grand Old Party to usher in 21st-century Republicanism. The leaders of the new ruling party will be doing themselves, their party, and their nation a huge disservice if they think they were given free rein to inflict their philosophy on the American public. Rather, voters spoke loudly that they want a restoration of fiscal and political sanity to Washington.

As such, the Republicans will earn their leadership role if they are willing to make hard decisions for the betterment of the country. Some of these choices, such as raising certain taxes in a targeted and temporary way and cutting programs where necessary, will be hugely unpopular across the board as we have seen in Wisconsin and New Jersey. Cutting taxes, particularly on the corporate level, may prove divisive, particularly among those who have decided the best way to capitalize on the national mood is to wage class warfare. But these decisions must be made, accompanied by the willingness to sacrifice short-term political gain for long-term national prosperity.

As for investors, the key will be to keep heart and stay cautious. People make money in all types of economic climates, and this will be no exception. Many will be focused on simply holding onto capital as we navigate this landscape, and that for sure should command strong attention in portfolios. Yet a willingness to take on hard assets—precious metals such as gold, as well as real estate and related classes—provide solid returns historically when confronted with similar circumstances. Oil prices are likely to shoot higher, and investors should be ready there as well. And holding Treasury Inflation Protected Securities, or TIPS, will be essential.

Mostly, though, investors will need to take the long view while we go through this crisis, as we unfortunately suspect that the political and policy changes needed to get us through could be slow to come by.

Dallas Fed Chief Fisher, in the aforementioned speech, went on to describe a nightmare scenario of "appearing before the House

Banking Committee in 2012 to report that the central bank of the United States has generated a loss of 'X' billion dollars." He worried that the Fed's money-cheapening policies were doing little more than encouraging excessive risk taking and speculation in the financial markets, benefiting deep-pocketed market players while penalizing savers and others on the periphery. But ultimately, when the inevitable day of reckoning comes to call, the Fed policies will have accomplished "transferring income from the poor and the worker and the saver to the rich. Senior citizens and others who saved and played by the rules are earning nothing on their savings, while big debtors and too-big-to-fail oligopoly banks benefit from their subsidy."[9]

Yet this seems the path on which the central bank is walking, gambling that inflation will not become so pernicious as to eat away at the real value of the Treasuries it is buying, so much so that even coupon payments on the bonds do not generate enough revenue to cover the Fed's capital losses. To hear an epistemically arrogant doomsday prophet espouse such sentiment on television would be one thing; to hear it from an influential member of the Federal Reserve Open Market Committee is chilling.

Fisher rightly said it would only take a situation in which "unreasonable scenarios prevail." Remember Taleb's Black Swan warnings of "the highly improbable consequential event" that is not foreseen due to "the scandal of prediction"?

We have been here before.

Notes

Chapter 1

1. "U.S. Treasury Debt Position and Activity Report," September 2010. Also, "U.S. Treasury. Bureau of Economic Analysis—Gross Domestic Product," U.S. Treasury. www.bea.gov/national/index.htm#gdp, www.treasurydirect.gov/govt/reports/pd/pd_debtposactrpt_1009.pdf
2. Laffer, Arthur, Moore, Stephen, and Tanous, Peter. *The End of Prosperity: How Higher Taxes Will Doom the Economy—If We Let It Happen* (New York: Simon & Schuster, 2009).
3. Barr, Alistair. "Hayman Hedge Fund's Chief: Currency War, Defaults Lie Ahead," Dow Jones Newswires, Oct. 13, 2010.
4. Fisher, Daniel. "The Global Debt Bomb," *Forbes*, Feb. 8, 2010.
5. "Federal Debt and the Risk of a Fiscal Crisis," Congressional Budget Office, July 27, 2010. www.cbo.gov/ftpdocs/116xx/doc11659/07-27_Debt_FiscalCrisis_Brief.pdf
6. Graham, Jed. "U.S. Debt Shock May Hit in 2018, Maybe as Soon as 2013: Moody's," *Investor's Business Daily*, May 5, 2010. www.investors.com/NewsAndAnalysis/Article.aspx?id=532490
7. Reinhart, Carmen M., and Rogoff, Kenneth S. *This Time Is Different: Eight Centuries of Financial Folly* (Princeton, NJ: Princeton University Press, 2009).

Chapter 2

1. Feldenkirchen, Markus, Reiermann, Christian, Suaga, Michael, and Schlamp, Hans-Jürgen. "Fighting on All Fronts—Merkel Takes on the EU and Her Own Finance Minister," Spiegel Online International, March 22, 2010. www.spiegel.de/international/germany/0,1518,684968,00.html.
2. According to the European Union's Stability and Growth Pact, adopted in 1997, member countries pledged their budget deficits would not exceed 3 percent of GDP. http://ec.europa.eu/economy_finance/sgp/index_en.html
3. 2010 International Monetary Fund. "Greece: Second Review Under the Stand-By Arrangement—Staff Report; Press Release on the Executive Board Discussion; and Statement by the Executive Director for Greece." December 2010. www.imf.org/external/pubs/ft/scr/2010/cr10372.pdf
4. "Greece: Staff Report on Request for Stand-By Arrangement," International Monetary Fund. www.imf.org/external/pubs/ft/scr/2010/cr10110.pdf
5. "Greece may get 11-yr period to repay bailout—IMF," Reuters, Nov. 27, 2010.
6. Spiegal, Peter, and Gerrit Wiesmann. "Eurozone eyes bond buy-back plan." *Financial Times*, Jan. 20, 2011.
7. Fottrell, Quentin. "Irish Government Moves to Safeguard Banking System," Dow Jones Newswires, Sept. 30, 2008.
8. Fottrell, Quentin. "Govt: EUR7 Billion Recapitalization for AIB, Bank of Ireland," Dow Jones Newswires, Feb. 11, 2009.
9. Pogatchinik, Shawn. "Ireland's Prime Minister Fights Back over Handling of Economic Crisis, Vows to Stay as Leader," Associated Press, Dec. 8, 2010.
10. "Irish Unemployment Steady at 13.4 Percent: Official Data," Agence France-Presse, March 31, 2010.
11. "Irish 2014 Deficit Target 'Worryingly Ambitious,'" Dow Jones Newswires, Oct. 20, 2010.
12. Nixon, Simon. "Trichet Still Not Blinking," *Wall Street Journal*, Dec. 3, 2010.
13. Ross-Thomas, Emma. "Spain Holds First Strike since 2002 as Europe Marches," Bloomberg News, Sept. 29, 2010.
14. Brown, Matthew, and Ross-Thomas, Emma. "Spain's Credit Set for Moody's Cut as Economy Suffers," Bloomberg News, Sept. 29, 2010.
15. "Spain Braced for General Strike, but Impact May Be Limited," Agence France-Presse, Sept. 26, 2010.

16. "Economic Outlook for the Euro Area in 2010 and 2011," European Forecasting Network, Autumn 2010. www.eui.eu/Documents/RSCAS/Research/EFN/Reports/EFN2010autumn.pdf

17. Davies, Nigel. "Spain Sells 4bln at Bond Auctions, Yields Drop," Reuters, Sept. 16, 2010.

Chapter 3

1. McNichol, Elizabeth, Oliff, Phill, and Johnson, Nicholas. "States Continue to Feel Recession's Impact," Center on Budget and Policy Priorities. Oct. 7, 2010. www.cbpp.org/cms/?fa=view&id=711
2. Kelly, Kate. "More Cities on Brink of Bankruptcy," CNBC.com, May 26, 2010. www.cnbc.com/id/37354955/More_Cities_on_Brink_of_Bankruptcy
3. Ibid.
4. Ibid.
5. "Harrisburg Incinerator Fiasco Deserves an Investigation to Understand How It Happened," by *Harrisburg Patriot-News* Editorial Board, April 12, 2010. www.pennlive.com/editorials/index.ssf/2010/04/how_did_it_happen_incinerator.html
6. Pennsylvania Governor's Budget Office, www.portal.state.pa.us/portal/server.pt/community/office_of_the_budget____home/4408
7. Peters, Joey. "A Growing Pile of Debt for State Unemployment Insurance Programs," stateline.org, Aug. 4, 2010. www.stateline.org/live/details/story?contentId=503104
8. Paul, Ron. "The Inflation Tax," July 18, 2006. www.lewrockwell.com/paul/paul334.html. The original citation on house.gov has been taken down but this piece has been cited in numerous places across the Internet.
9. Center on Budget and Policy Priorities.
10. Merrick, Amy, Dougherty, Conor, and Wessel, David. "States Offer Washington Lesson in Belt Tightening," *Wall Street Journal*, Nov. 17, 2010.
11. Ibid.
12. Stateline.org. www.stateline.org/live/details/story?contentId=503104.
13. Chicago Fed report, 3Q/2010. www.chicagofed.org/digital_assets/publications/economic_perspectives/2010/3qtr2010_part1_mattoon_haleco%20meyer_foster.pdf
14. "Myth vs. Facts in Municipal Aid," State of New Jersey governor blog, Gov. Chris Christie. www.state.nj.us/governor/blog/20100414.shtml

15. "The Christie Reform Agenda: Taking Action to Provide Real Property Tax Relief," State of New Jersey, newsroom. www.state.nj.us/governor/news/news/552010/approved/20100510c.html

Chapter 4

1. "The Edict on Maximum Prices," translation from Forum Ancient Coins. www.forumancientcoins.com/numiswiki/view.asp?key=Edict%20of%20Diocletian%20Edict%20on%20Prices
2. "Jimmy Carter Vs. Inflation," *Time*, March 24, 1980. www.time.com/time/magazine/article/0,9171,921854-1,00.html
3. *Paul Volcker: The Making of a Financial Legend*, by Joseph B. Treaster (Hoboken, NJ: John Wiley & Sons, 2004), p. ix.
4. Hanke, Stephen H. "R.I.P. Zimbabwe Dollar," Cato Institute, May 3, 2010. www.cato.org/zimbabwe
5. "U.S. Inflation to Approach Zimbabwe Level, Faber Says," Bloomberg.com, May 27, 2009. www.bloomberg.com/apps/news?pid=newsarchive&sid=avgZDYM6mTFA
6. Pento, Michael. "Don't Lose Sleep over Deflation," Euro Pacific Capital, July 28, 2010. www.europac.net/commentaries/don%E2%80%99t_lose_sleep_over_deflation

Chapter 5

1. White, Aoife. "Eurozone Nations $1 Trillion Bailout Fund," Associated Press, June 7, 2010.
2. Wearden, Graeme. "Europe Bank's Stress Tests—As It Happened," *The Guardian*, July 23, 2010. www.guardian.co.uk/business/2010/jul/23/stress-tests-european-banks

Chapter 6

1. "Federal Debt and the Risk of a Fiscal Crisis," Congressional Budget Office, July 27, 2010.
2. "Federal Debt and Interest Costs," Congressional Budget Office, December 2010.
3. Congressional Budget Office, July 27, 2010.
4. Rogoff, Kenneth, and Reinhart, Carmen. "*Growth in a Time of Debt*," Harvard University Press, Feb. 24, 2010. www.economics.harvard.edu/faculty/rogoff/files/RR-Financial%20crash_February_241.pdf
5. Gordon, Robert J. *Productivity, Growth, Inflation and Unemployment*. (London: Cambridge University Press, 2004), p. 220.

Chapter 7

1. "Four Governors on How to Cut Spending," *Wall Street Journal*, Oct. 13, 2010.
2. "Fiscal Policy Report Card on America's Governors," Cato Institute, Sept. 30, 2010. www.cato.org/pubs/pas/PA668.pdf
3. AAA Fuel Gauge Report. http://fuelgaugereport.aaa.com/
4. Carroll, Daniel, and Mowry, Beth. "Personal Savings Up, National Savings Down." Federal Reserve of Cleveland, March 19, 2010. www.clevelandfed.org/research/trends/2010/0410/01ecoact.cfm
5. Roubini, Nouriel. *Crisis Economics: A Crash Course in the Future of Finance* (New York: Penguin, 2010), p. 258.
6. "The Economy and Why the Federal Reserve Needs to Supervise Banks," Feb. 16, 2010. Narayana Kocherlokota in speech to Minnesota Bankers Association. www.minneapolisfed.org/news_events/pres/speech_display.cfm?id=4388
7. Shlaes, Amity. *The Forgotten Man: A New History of the Great Depression* (New York: Harper Perennial, 2008), p. 13.

Chapter 8

1. Chan, Sewell. "Fed Chief Defends Action in Face of Criticism," *New York Times*, Nov. 5, 2010. www.nytimes.com/2010/11/06/business/economy/06fed.html?_r=2&ref=business
2. Medved, Michael. *The 5 Big Lies about American Business: Combating Smears against the Free-Market Economy*. (New York: Crown Forum, 2009), p. 31.
3. Mitchell, Daniel. "The Historical Lessons of Lower Tax Rates," Heritage Foundation, Aug. 13, 2003. www.heritage.org/research/reports/2003/08/the-historical-lessons-of-lower-tax-rates
4. Ibid.
5. Ibid.
6. Ibid.
7. Ibid.
8. "Corporate Taxes and Economic Growth," PricewaterhouseCoopers, Feb. 1, 2010. www.techceocouncil.org/storage/documents/Corporate_taxes_and_Economic_Growth_FEB.pdf
9. Pento, Michael. "Does the Fed Create Money?" Forbes.com, Nov. 22, 2010. http://blogs.forbes.com/michaelpento/
10. PricewaterhouseCoopers.
11. Ibid.

12. Dubay, Curtis. "Value Added Tax: No Easy Fix for the Deficit," Heritage Foundation, January 21, 2010. www.heritage.org/research/reports/2010/01/value-added-tax-no-easy-fix-for-the-deficit

13. "Volcker on the VAT," *Wall Street Journal* Editorial Board, April 8, 2010. http://online.wsj.com/article/SB10001424052702303720604575170320672253834.html

14. Houtzager, Mark. "Reagan's Economic Adviser Supports Supports a U.S. VAT." www.us-vat.com/blog/?p=241

15. Bach, Richard. *Illusions: The Adventures of a Reluctant Messiah* (New York: Dell 1989).

16. Times Higher Education Survey. "World Reputation Rankings 2011." www.timeshighereducation.co.uk/world-university-rankings/

17. Wolfe, Patrick J. "School Voucher Programs: What the Research Says about Parental School Choice," *Brigham Young University Law Review*, July 8, 2008. www.redorbit.com/news/technology/1467036/school_voucher_programs_what_the_research_says_about_parental_school/

Chapter 9

1. Keynes, John Maynard. *A Tract on Monetary Reform* (1923). (New York: Prometheus Book, 2000), p. 80.

2. "Exploiting Generational Anomalies in Stock vs. Bond Returns," Leuthol Group, 2009.

Chapter 10

1. According to data on CNBC.com. http://data.cnbc.com/quotes/GCCV1.

2. "Gold Is Still 33% Below Its Inflation Adjusted 1980 Peak," Gold Investments, www.marketoracle.co.uk/Article2248.html

3. Artigas, Juan Carlos. "Linking Global Money Supply to Gold and to Future Inflation," World Gold Council, February 2010.

4. Pento, Michael "Gold's Allure Tied to Interest rates," Forbes.com, Nov. 17, 2010. http://blogs.forbes.com/michaelpento/2010/11/17/golds-allure-tied-to-interest-rates/

Chapter 11

1. Yergin, Daniel. *The Prize: The Epic Quest for Oil, Money, and Power* (New York: Simon & Schuster, 2008).

2. Tanous, Peter J. "The Investment Case for Energy and Oil," December 2006.

Chapter 12

1. Gauss, Carl Friedrich. *Disquisitiones Arithmeticae.* Translated by Arthur A. Clarke (Yale University Press, 1965); Hall, Tord. *Carl Friedrich Gauss: A Biography* (Cambridge, MA: MIT Press, 1970).
2. Louis Bachelier Bio, www-groups.dcs.st-and.ac.uk/~history/Biographies/Bachelier.html; referred from Bachelier Finance Society, http://www.bachelierfinance.org/
3. Harry Markowitz Autobiography, Official Web Site of the Nobel Prize, http://nobelprize.org/nobel_prizes/economics/laureates/1990/markowitz-autobio.html
4. Hoffman, Jascha. "Benoit Mandelbrot, Novel Mathematician, Dies at 85," *New York Times,* Oct. 16, 2010. www.nytimes.com/2010/10/17/us/17mandelbrot.html
5. Taleb accepts fractal geometry as a means to reject the Gaussian, but not as a way to compute risks of market events.
6. Taleb, *The Black Swan* (New York: Random House, 2007), pp. 229–230.
7. Mandelbrot, Benoit. *The (Mis)behavior of Markets* (New York: Basic Books, 2004), p. 97.
8. Mandelbrot, Benoit. *The Fractal Geometry of Nature* (New York: W.H. Freeman, 1983), p. xiii.

Conclusion

1. Huntley, Jonathan. "Federal Debt and the Risk of a Fiscal Crisis," Congressional Budget Office. www.cbo.gov/ftpdocs/116xx/doc11659/07-27_Debt_FiscalCrisis_Brief.pdf
2. Greenblatt, Alan. "The Federal Debt: How to Lose a Trillion Dollars," NPR, April 30, 2010. www.npr.org/templates/story/story.php?storyId=126413824
3. Ibid.
4. Ibid.
5. "The Federal Government's Long-Term Fiscal Outlook Fall 2010 Update," www.scribd.com/doc/42937254/The-Federal-Government%E2%80%99s-Long-Term-Fiscal-Outlook-Fall-2010-Update
6. Taleb, *The Black Swan.* (New York: Random House, 2007).
7. Weisenthal, Joe. "Dallas Fed Chief: The Fed is Monetizing the Nation's Debt for the Next Eight Months," BusinessInsider.com, Nov. 8, 2010. www.businessinsider.com/dalls-fed-chief-fisher-debt-monetization-2010-11

8. Cox, Jeff. "No Inflation: Grocery Stores, Gas Prices Tell Different Story," CNBC.com, Nov. 12, 2010. www.cnbc.com/id/40132000/No_Inflation_Grocery_Stores_Gas_Prices_Tell_Different_Story
9. Weisenthal. "Dallas Fed Chief."

Acknowledgments

From both of us: Thanks to our agent, Theron Raines, and our superb editors, Debby Englander, Emilie Herman, Stacey Fischkelta, Adrianna Johnson, and all the other many talented people at John Wiley & Sons who contributed so much to this book.

In addition, each of us had support in our individual work on this book and we want to express our gratitude.

From Peter Tanous: Thanks for help and advice from (my hero) Nassim Nicholas Taleb; Miroslav Kollar; Vipin Sahijwani, CFA; Brian Conway; Arthur B. Laffer; Douglas H. Ginsburg; Thierry Callault; Zachery Kouwe; Francois Letaconnoux and all my colleagues at Lepercq Lynx Investment Advisory; and a special shout-out to Katie Fleiss, CFA, who provided invaluable assistance and support throughout the process of writing the book. Thanks to my talented co-author Jeff Cox with whom it has been a pleasure to work.

From Jeff Cox: This project simply could not have been completed without the tremendous support of so many of my colleagues at CNBC.com and CNBC television. Thanks in particular to Allen Wastler and Scott Billings for their time, patience, and indulgence. Also, to Michael Pento for his support and ideas. Thanks as well to the many sources I've called on to contribute to my understanding of capital markets, in particular Quincy Krosby, Kathy Boyle, Michael Cohn, Nadav Baum, and of course, my esteemed co-author Peter. I will always be indebted for the time and patience of the many people who helped formulate the ideas that made this book possible.

About the Authors

Peter J. Tanous is President of Lepercq Lynx Advisory of Washington, D.C., an SEC-registered investment advisory consulting firm. A graduate of Georgetown University, he serves on the university's investment committee. Mr. Tanous' book, *Investment Gurus*, published by Prentice Hall in 1997, received wide critical acclaim in financial circles and was chosen as a main selection of The Money Book Club. Other books include *The Wealth Equation* (Prentice Hall Press, 1999), *Investment Visionaries* (Penguin Group, 2003), and *Kiplinger's Build a Winning Portfolio* (Kaplan Publishing, 2008). He co-authored (with Dr. Arthur Laffer and Stephen Moore) *The End of Prosperity*, published by Simon & Schuster in October 2008. Peter Tanous serves on several corporate and nonprofit boards of directors. He lives in Washington. D.C. with his wife, Ann.

Jeff Cox has been a journalist since 1987 and currently covers the markets and economy for CNBC.com and appears on CNBC broadcast. He also provides guest commentary for radio stations across the country, and his work has appeared in numerous publications and Web sites including TheStreet.com, Yahoo Finance, and *USA Today*. Prior to coming to CNBC he worked at CNNMoney and before that as a senior editor and columnist for Pennsylvania newspapers. His work has been honored by the Pennsylvania Newspaper Association and New Jersey Press Association, and he has been a speaker at Columbia University's journalism program. A Pennsylvania native, he is a graduate of Bloomsburg University and lives in Lower Mount Bethel, along the Delaware River, with his wife, MaryEllen.

Index